BIRDS
OF THE
CAYMAN ISLANDS

PATRICIA BRADLEY

BIRDS
OF THE
CAYMAN ISLANDS

PHOTOGRAPHY
YVES-JACQUES
REY-MILLET

FOREWORD
H.R.H. THE DUKE OF EDINBURGH
K.G., K.T.

PREFACE
DR. OSCAR OWRE PH.D.

First edition 1985
Revised edition 1995

Published by Caerulea Press, Italy.

ISBN 976–8052–10–4

Phototypesetting and Colour Separations by
Create Publishing Services Limited, Bath

Printed in England by Bath Press Colourbooks, Glasgow

The Land Fund of the National Trust for the Cayman Islands
benefits from the sale of this book.

The author wishes to thank the Chief Surveyor, Lands and
Survey, Cayman Islands Government for his kind permission
to reproduce the maps of the Cayman Islands.

FRONT COVER: Cuban Parrot, Cayman Brac sub-
                      species *(Amazona leucocephala hesterna)*
BACK COVER: West Indian Whistling-Ducks *(Dendro-
                      cygna arborea)*
PHOTOGRAPHS BY THE AUTHOR: Plates 2, 5, 7, 8,
                      15, 16, 17, 22, 27, 32, 38

THIS BOOK IS
LOVINGLY DEDICATED TO
TWO MICHAELS

P.E.B.

TO MY GRANDMOTHER
AND ANNE-MARIE

Y.J.R.M.

CONTENTS

APPENDIX 3

BIBLIOGRAPHY

ENGLISH AND LATIN INDEX

FOREWORD
H.R.H. THE DUKE OF EDINBURGH K.G., K.T.

BUCKINGHAM PALACE.

The first step towards active conservation is knowledge and understanding of nature's problems. Bird-watching and recognition may seem like a gentle hobby but it is much more than that. It is a window onto the natural world and with growing experience it is possible to appreciate what is happening to indigenous and migratory bird populations. This in turn leads to a better understanding of the major issues of the conservation of nature.

I hope that this book will encourage many people to take an intelligent interest in the birds of the Cayman Islands and I hope it will also provide an introduction to the problems of nature conservation both in the Cayman Islands and worldwide.

1984.

LIST OF PLATES

PREFACE TO THE FIRST EDITION

Birds of the Cayman Islands is a noteworthy publication. The first field guide to direct entire attention to the birds of three smallish Islands, islands which for many are crossroads of the Caribbean, it will be greeted with delight by natural history buffs of all persuasions, visitors to the islands, students and people with curious intent.

"A first step towards knowledge", so goes an old saying, "is learning the names of things". To those who enjoy their gardens and natural places, acquaintance with the avifauna is compelling. To learn the names of birds you must, of course, be able to recognize them. Patricia Bradley's field guide makes "This first step towards knowledge" an easy one.

The guide leads you further than just naming the birds you meet. It will tease your imagination in special ways. Where have these Islands' birds come from? Ancestors of the permanent residents obviously colonized the Cayman Islands long ago — long enough ago that some now differ in various ways from their close relatives of other land masses. Knowing ranges of relatives and inspecting maps, one begins hypothesizing the origins of the Cayman Islands' residents. Some birds spend only the summer here, some only the winter; the field guide identifies their "other" homes. Some are irregular wanderers (potential colonizers?) from neighbouring or even distant land. Some only pause here while en route between their winter and summer ranges. Some are waifs from the sea itself. Tutored with such information about each species, the reader is started on the way to thinking biogeographically.

The field guide also offers opportunities. Avifaunal lists for islands always await additions. To be sure, there are not apt to be additions to the list of island residents. Additional records of uncommonly seen birds, however, are much needed — maybe they are not as uncommon as we now think or maybe there are cycles of occurrence. And unrecorded species — migrants, wanderers, waifs — can cross the islands' horizons at any time. By reporting their observations, careful bird watchers can contribute to our knowledge of the Cayman Islands' birds.

Every island is a unique world. Who, whether an island

dweller or a visitor, can be immune from the excitement of exploring for animals of a unique world? Here is a field guide that will nourish anticipation. Then it will introduce you expertly and neatly to all of the Islands' known birds.

Oscar T. Owre
Maytag Professor of Ornithology Emeritus
and Professor of Biology, University of Miami.
1984.

ACKNOWLEDGMENTS

It is with deep gratitude and delight I wish to thank His Royal Highness, The Duke of Edinburgh, for graciously agreeing to write the Foreword to this book. His lifelong commitment to the preservation of wildlife throughout our planet is well known and this letter demonstrates his continuing interest in the Cayman Islands.

To Dr. Oscar Owre, who wrote the Preface, I offer my heartfelt thanks. He has generously given time to a detailed reading of the manuscript and all his pertinent recommendations and criticisms have greatly strengthened the text. He has shared his superb library and answered long distance pleas for information and advice with a gentle patience and unfailing good humour. It has been a great privilege to work with him.

This book is a combined result of many hours in the field and at the desk and of willing help given by so many people in the Islands and beyond. To them all I offer my grateful thanks and appreciation. I should like to acknowledge with gratitude my debt to Dr. Marco Giglioli, for providing the information needed to begin writing the book; he is sadly missed.

I wish to thank the following for sharing their expertise: Dr. David Johnston, Dr. James Bond, Dr. Howard Teas, Dr. Wesley Lanyon, Audrey Downer, Alick Moore and David Wingate.

My warmest thanks to the following for help and assistance in many fields: Dr. Alan Milner, Fred Burton, Dr. Jim Wood, Tony Fenton, Rudolph Davis, Derek Banks, Miss Elo Estaban, E.J., Gloria Williams, Mark Latham, Captain Mabry Kirkconnell, Ruth and Johnny Fisher, Maureen Collins, Anne-Marie Rey-Millet, Barbara Cargill, Twink Scarborough, Simon Barwick, Kearney Gomez, Viv Pearce, and all at the Southern Cross Club, Little Cayman, especially Mike Emmanuel and Bert Ebanks. My thanks also to Mrs. St. Aubyn and the late Mr. Bernard St. Aubyn and Mr. and Mrs. Kassa.

Thank you to fellow birders for sharing field records: Brenda Quinn, the late Ira Thompson, Willie Ebanks, Charles Adams, Rudi Powery, Dorian Miller and Mars Van

Liefde. My thanks also to Melbourne Watler, Stacey Watler, Vernon Jackson and Allan and Louise Dibben for their help in locating Whistling-Duck.

My grateful thanks to Ruth Smested-Anglin and Lorrain Ebanks for their patience and skill in typing the endless drafts of the manuscript and to Mary Gillooly for proof-reading and final editing. It has been a pleasure to work with World-Wide Printing and I am grateful for their efforts to ensure, at long distance, that this book was produced as we requested.

Finally, to my son Michael, my love and a big thank you for his help with bird calls, his observations, and so much patience. To my husband Michael, my special gratitude and love. His assistance and support in every aspect of the field work and writing, including editing and proof-reading, has been a continuing inspiration.

P.E.B. 1984

The photographer would like to respectfully thank H.R.H. The Prince Philip, Duke of Edinburgh, for so kindly writing the Foreword. He is also very grateful to Mrs. Bradley who so generously shared with him her knowledge of the islands best birding places. He would like to emphasize that working with her on this project has been an extremely instructive and pleasurable experience. He would like to thank Mrs. Jacqueline Schobel, Mrs. Faith Black, Dr. Arnold Small, Mr. John Rudolph, Dr. Lear Grimmer, Mr. Terry Berykczynski, Loxley Gould, Mervyn Cumber and all the others who helped with the photographs for this volume. A special thank-you to Peter Jackson, Mr. Richard Hamilton and Michelle Depraz of WWF.

Y.J.R.M. 1984

THE REVISED EDITION

It is ten years since the first edition went to press. Our knowledge of Cayman birds has increased greatly with data collected during my field-work for an annotated check-list, and censuses of the islands waterfowl and of the amazon parrots. New records and information have also come from Michael Marsden and members of the Cayman Islands Bird Club of Grand Cayman, and Keith Prescott and Dr. Jim Wiley in Cayman Brac. I wish to thank them all for generously sharing their field notes.

I wish to express my thanks to His Royal Highness, The Duke of Edinburgh, for graciously agreeing to the reprinting of his Foreward to the first edition. Special thanks also to Maureen and John Collins and Mary and Ben Gillooly in Grand Cayman and Gladys Howard of Pirates Point, Little Cayman for their warm hospitality and the loan of vehicles during my field work for the revision. My thanks also to Dr Richard Banks, Dr George Reynard, Marie Martin, the National Trust for the Cayman Islands, Fred Burton, Jeff Kerforth and Cris Evans. I am indebted to John Bebb for help with maps and Michael Marsden for critical comments on the text. I wish to thank Create Publishing Services, especially Doug Hilditch, for their very professional approach. It has been a delight to work with them.

My special gratitude to two Michaels for their dedication and real support: to my son for literary polish and proofing and cross-referencing the index and to my husband for what must have seemed unending crepuscular hours formatting and proof-reading the drafts, especially after a similar diurnal exercise. I could not have done it without them.

In 1991, Oscar Owre died. As a legacy this gifted and inspired teacher left several generations of dedicated ornithologists, scattered far and wide, to continue his quest to understand and protect the natural world; they and his many friends continue to miss him.

The underlying purpose of the guide remains threefold: to display the richness of our Islands' birds, to demonstrate their dependance on chosen habitats, and to encourage the people of the Islands to require that protection is extended to sufficient areas of unspoilt wetland and terrestrial habitat to ensure the survival of the indigenous plants and animals. The rewards for increased care and commitment, however, are without measure. Everyone stands to benefit from a healthy natural environment because it guarantees the well-being of present and future generations in the Cayman Islands.

P.E.B.
Grand Cayman 1995.

INTRODUCTION TO THE REVISED EDITION

This edition of the guide updates the status of all known Cayman Islands' birds and their habitats. It describes all breeding species and adds many new records to the original list of winter and passage migrants, casual and vagrant visitors. Recent exotics and recently extinct species are also included. The introduction relates how the position and biogeography of the Islands determines the composition and seasonal patterns of the avifauna, and how a recognition of the different habitats points to where species are most likely to occur in each Island. Designed for use in Grand Cayman (GC), Little Cayman (LC) and Cayman Brac (CB), the guide clarifies variations in the avifauna between the three Islands. It aims to reach both residents and tourists, experts and amateurs, to ensure their birding experiences in the field become easier and more enjoyable.

Cayman birds have been studied since 1886 when collections were described by Cory. In the following one hundred years many ornithologists and collectors have visited the Islands for brief periods. In 1982, I became resident in Grand Cayman and began regular visits in all months to Cayman Brac and Little Cayman. For the first time comparative monthly records for the three Islands were available and this book is the result of those studies. Also, being the first field guide, attention and resources were directed towards studies of the forty-six species of breeding birds. The resulting text, combined with photographs taken in habitats throughout the three Islands, is a unique record of this avifauna as well as contributing to our knowledge of birds in the Greater Antilles. Photographs of North American species are omitted as they have been exhaustively illustrated in summer and winter plumage in several excellent West Indian and North American field guides recommended in the Bibliography. Appendix 1 gives a check-list of breeding birds. Appendix 2 lists vagrant, very rare and introduced species. Appendix 3 contains information on the best birding locations, new maps of the three Islands marking the main roads, lakes and ponds, the extent of the mangrove and a map showing the position of the Cayman Islands in the Caribbean Sea. Finally there is a Bibliography and an Index.

Facts on the biogeography of the Cayman Islands

Position.   Between 19°20′ and 19°43′ north and 81°21′ and 79°50′ west, the Islands lie at the extreme northwest end of Caribbean island chain, 280km (174 miles) from Jamaica and 240km (149 miles) from Cuba. Grand Cayman lies 117km (73 miles) west-southwest of Little Cayman, which is 7.5km (5 miles) due west of Cayman Brac.

Land Area

Total	263km²; 99 sq. miles.
Grand Cayman	197km²; 76 sq. miles.
Cayman Brac	38km²; 13 sq. miles.
Little Cayman	28km²; 10 sq. miles.

Climate

Temperature	average 25°C; 77°F. Range 14°-36°C; 57°-97°F.
Humidity	average 75%.
Rainfall	average GC = 1351mm; CB = 1112mm; LC = 1174mm; wet season May to November.
Winds	mainly northeast trades in winter, with occasional northwesterly storms. East-southeast trades in summer.
Tides	average 26cm; 10in or a maximum 60 cm; 24in. Rivers and streams are absent.

Elevation

Max. Grand Cayman	19m; 62ft.
Max. Cayman Brac	44m; 144ft.
Max. Little Cayman	13m; 43ft.

Geology   The three islands are carbonate outcrops of the Cayman Ridge, a submarine mountain range extending from Cuba to Central America. The Ridge forms the northern margin of the Cayman Trough, which reaches depths in excess of 6,000m. The three Islands were lifted above sea-level in the middle Miocene and each is thought to be located on separate fault blocks thus allowing independent movement. The central core of each Island is Bluff Formation, a dense crystalline dolostone (carbonate), formed in the late Oligocene period (circa 30 million years old) and exposed as the marine cliffs of Grand Cayman and Cayman Brac. The youngest rocks date from the Pliocene, about 2 million years ago. The surface of the Formation is a karst, with honey-combed pinnacles, sink-holes and fissures on which the associated woodland and bushland maintain a seemingly precarious existence. Underlying the Formation is an extensive cave system. Exploring this area is only possible using roads, tracks, survey cuts or old footpaths. Surrounding the Bluff limestone core is a low (max. 5m) coastal platform of Pleistocene Ironshore, about 125,000 years old, which was formed during the last interglacial period. This fine textured limestone rock is a marine consolidation of sand, coral, molluscs and lagoonal mud. Between 5,000 to 3,000 years ago in the mid-Holocene period, the sea level rose to 1 metre below the present level and the mangrove swamps developed to their present extent. Ironshore, underlying plastic mud and Holocene peats form much of the western part of Grand Cayman, including the Central Mangrove Swamp, and a low platform around Cayman Brac and eastern Little Cayman.

Ecosystems   Grand Cayman and Little Cayman are similar low-lying islands with extensive wetlands of mangrove swamps and associated coastal lagoons and ponds, covering around 35% of the land area of Grand Cayman and 25% of Little Cayman. This ecosystem is associated with the Ironshore Platform rock. Only Grand Cayman has freshwater wetlands including ponds, flooded grassland, brackish cat-tail swamp and sedge ponds. In Cayman Brac the wetlands are minimal, confined to the southwest.

The extensive coastal (littoral) ecosystem on the three islands includes the fringing reef, the shore of sandy beach or Ironshore, and the band of woodland or bushland behind the shore.

The third ecosystem is the terrestrial vegetation of woodland and bushland associated with the Bluff Formation in the three Islands. In Cayman Brac this accounts for 75% of the land area, where the bluff rises in the west, ascends to 44 metres in the extreme east and terminates in marine cliffs.

The Avifauna

Derivation The endemic West Indian avifauna is believed to be derived from southern North American stock during the Tertiary era. The West Indian islands are oceanic and are thought never to have been connected by land-bridges to mainland America. Birds first colonized the Greater Antilles on the wing, island-hopping from coastal Central America during periods of lowered sea-level (plants and animals also colonized by rafting). Once in the islands successful colonizers needed to be highly mobile, fast breeders and flexible in choice of habitat to become established. Later development into island endemics took place due to geographic isolation. Fossils dated from the late Pleistocene to the early Holocene from cave deposits in Grand Cayman and Cayman Brac point to an earlier extinct avifauna with an intra-island distribution different from that of today (Morgan, Bibliog.). Fossils of species now extinct include two raptors, a giant West Indian hawk and a Caracara, and a second species of bullfinch. Fossils of species still occurring in adjacent islands include Audubon's Shearwater, White Ibis, Clapper Rail, Plain Pigeon, Lizard Cuckoo, Burrowing Owl and Cuban Crow.

The present Cayman Islands avifauna is derived from that of Jamaica and Cuba with 63% of landbirds shared with those two islands. The closest affinity is with Cuba with six species shared exclusively. The Caribbean Elaenia, *Elaenia martinica*, is the only representative from the Lesser Antilles. A few later colonizers were from North America, the result either of failed return migrations or of post-breeding

24

dispersals. In the present avifauna, while many of the endemic sub-species were known to exist as early as 8–10,000 years ago, all endemic species of landbirds are now extinct (the last in the 1930s); also there are no sub-species of waterfowl. This composition of the avifauna is determined by the small size of the three islands, by their low relief and limited habitat diversity, all factors which reduce the number of available niches. It supports the MacArthur Theory that the avifauna on small oceanic islands is unstable, noted for a high species turnover with immigrations balanced by extinctions, a feature tending to reduce endemism.

The present avifauna, excluding vagrants and introduced species, comprises 34 families, 105 genera, over 200 species and 17 endemic sub-species. Within the last 20 years several exotic caged birds species have escaped or were deliberately introduced and four species have established small feral breeding populations.

Breeding birds   Forty-six species have been confirmed as breeding in the Islands since 1975, with one species, the Least Bittern, still unconfirmed as breeding (See Check-list, Appendix 1). Five species breed and are summer visitors only: the White-tailed Tropicbird (*Phaethon lepturus*), Least Tern (*Sterna antillarum*), Antillean Nighthawk (*Chordeiles gundlachii*), Gray Kingbird (*Tyrannus dominicensis*) and Black-whiskered Vireo (*Vireo altiloquus*). The three landbirds winter in South America. Two new colonizers arrived comparatively recently: the White-winged Dove (*Zenaida asiatica*) about 1935 and the Cattle Egret (*Bubulcus ibis*) in 1957. The only endemic species, the Grand Cayman Thrush (*Turdus ravidus*), was last seen in 1938 and is regarded as extinct. The sub-species of the Jamaican Oriole (*Icterus leucopteryx bardi*) was last seen in 1967 and is now extirpated from the Cayman Islands' part of its range. The latter two species occurred in Grand Cayman only.

Landbirds   Twenty-eight species are presently breeding, though not all species breed on each Island; their distribution is shown in Appendix I. Twenty-five species breed in Grand Cayman. Six occur exclusively: the Caribbean Dove

Table 1. Check-list and distribution of endemic sub-species

Species	Grand Cayman	Cayman Brac	Little Cayman
Caribbean Dove			
Leptotila jamaicensis collaris	+		
Cuban Parrot			
Amazona leucocephala caymanensis	+		
A. l. hesterna		+	e
West Indian Woodpecker			
Melanerpes superciliaris caymanensis	+		
Northern Flicker			
Colaptes auratus gundlachi	+		
Caribbean Elaenia			
Elaenia martinica caymanensis	+	+	+
Loggerhead Kingbird			
Tyrannus caudifasciatus caymanensis	+	+	e
Red-legged Thrush			
Turdus plumbeus coryi		+	
Thick-billed Vireo			
Vireo crassirostris alleni	+	+	e
Yucatan Vireo			
Vireo magister caymanensis	+		
Vitelline Warbler			
Dendroica vitellina vitellina	+		
D. v. crawfordi		+	+
Bananaquit			
Coereba flaveola sharpei	+	+	+
Stripe-headed Tanager			
Spindalis zena salvini	+		
Cuban Bullfinch			
Melopyrrha nigra taylori	+		
Greater Antillean Grackle			
Quiscalus niger caymanensis	+		
Q. n. bangsi		e	+

Status : + = breeding recorded e = extirpated

(*Leptotila jamaicensis*), West Indian Woodpecker (*Melanerpes superciliaris*), Northern Flicker (*Colaptes auratus*), Yucatan Vireo (*Vireo magister*), Stripe-headed Tanager (*Spindalis zena*) and Cuban Bullfinch (*Melopyrrha nigra*).

One species, the Red-legged Thrush (*Turdus plumbeus*), breeds exclusively in Cayman Brac. Little Cayman has no exclusive species; presently only 17 species breed while the Loggerhead Kingbird (*Tyrannus caudifasciatus*), Thick-billed Vireo (*Vireo crassirostris*) and Cuban Parrot (*Amazona leucocephala*) have all become extirpated there. The Black-whiskered Vireo (*Vireo altiloquus*) and the Gray Kingbird (*Tyrannus dominicensis*) breed in summer in Cayman Brac and Little Cayman only.

A characteristic of several species is a wide habitat tolerance. For example, the Bananaquit (*Coererba flaveola*) is found in all habitats in the three Islands, feeds at all heights and is insectivorous, fructiverous and nectariverous, thus successfully occupying several niches and possibly excluding several colonizing species. According to Lack, this may account for the complete absence of hummingbirds, as the Cayman Islands and Mona (off Puerto Rico) are the only West Indian islands without a single species of that genus.

Endemic sub-species Genetic isolation has gradually led to sub-speciation, the first stage on the road to specific endemism. There are 17 endemic sub-species in the Cayman Islands: 13 in Grand Cayman (nine occur exclusively), seven in Cayman Brac (two occur exclusively) and four in Little Cayman (one occurs exclusively). The Cuban Parrot in Grand Cayman is *Amazona leucocephala caymanensis*, whereas the Cayman Brac sub-species is *Amazona leucocephala hesterna*. The Greater Antillean Grackle in Grand Cayman is *Quiscalus niger caymanensis;* in Little Cayman it is replaced by *Quiscalus niger bangsi* which has not been recorded in Cayman Brac since the 1960s. The sub-species of Vitelline Warbler in Grand Cayman is *Dendroica vitellina vitellina* and in Cayman Brac and Little Cayman it is *Dendroica vitellina crawfordi*.

Waterbirds Large colonies of Magnificent Frigatebirds and Red-footed Boobies breed in Little Cayman. Brown Boobies and White-tailed Tropicbirds breed in Cayman Brac (a small colony of the latter also breeds in Grand Cayman). The Least Tern is the only species of larid to breed in the three Islands in summer. Six species of heron breed, some only intermittently. To date the status of the resident Least Bittern remains unconfirmed in Grand Cayman, although breeding is probable and immatures are often seen, no eggs or juveniles have been observed. The only breeding resident duck, the West Indian Whistling-Duck, a Greater Antillean endemic, which had ceased to breed in Cayman Brac returned in 1993 after 12 years. Among the rails, only the Common Moorhen breeds in large numbers. The Purple Gallinule, which occurs throughout the Islands as a spring migrant, is only known to breed in Grand Cayman, and there is only a single record of the American Coot breeding. The common Black-necked Stilt breeds on the three Islands. The Willet breeds in small numbers in the three Islands; it is a fairly common migrant and the only species of shorebird to breed here.

Migrants The position of the Cayman Islands at the edge of the western flyway between North and South America is the reason for 75% of the avifauna occurring as migrants between their northern breeding grounds and their southern wintering grounds (where they spend up to nine months of the year). Spring and fall passage migrants account for the greatest species variety and abundance, while over-wintering migrants are fewer and in smaller populations, see page 46. Among the waterbirds, herons and shorebirds show the largest populations and species diversity. Among land-birds the warblers are by far the largest group with 19 species recorded regularly. Very rare passage migrants, casuals and vagrants already account for over 20% of migrants and new species continue to be added as interest in bird-watching grows. Some species, previously thought to be extremely rare, are now known to be of infrequent but regular occurrence. Other species, also of uncommon occurrence for many years, have been observed as locally common in a specific month, often as short-stay visitors in winter. So, beware, the status records for migrants refer to the *expected* numbers of regular migrants only!

Conservation

The endemic birds, animals and plants that colonized these remote Islands arrived by air and by sea many eons ago. Gradually they became established in the delicate and fragile ecosystems, despite the harsh terrain and lack of rivers and streams. Island systems are precarious. If a population of birds or plants is reduced to very small numbers replacement by reproduction becomes impossible resulting in the extinction of a unique form. Man's destruction of natural habitats, resulting in unacceptable competition for decreased space and food, is the single most damaging factor causing extinction of wild plant and animal species in the world today.

Threats to habitats With the arrival of the North American land boom in 1977, the problem reached the Cayman Islands. Grand Cayman has continued to develop rapidly with a concomitant growth of tourist hotels, marinas and golf courses mainly sited on filled mangrove swamp and cleared coastal woodland. Originally development was concentrated around George Town and north along Seven Mile Beach; now the rapidly increasing population (14,000 in 1980 to 30,000 in 1994) is expanding eastwards around the Central Mangrove Swamp and into the remaining terrestrial woodland. Habitats are becoming fragmented east of Savannah and, in a short time, this will be reflected in a decline in bird diversity as has already taken place in western Grand Cayman.

New zoning policies are required to protect sufficient areas of representative habitats to maintain the present avifauna in the three Islands. For example, the Central Mangrove Swamp is a vital area for Grand Cayman, supporting most of the breeding waterbirds, as well as parrots, vireos and migrant warblers, while its border with North Sound is the nursery for much of the marine life on our reefs. The entire Swamp urgently needs to be declared protected; the existing zoning is mainly for urban development. Up to 1988 Little Cayman was undeveloped: there was no electricity (or utility poles), no sealed roads and few vehicles. A rapid development of the infrastructure and of access by air has since allowed a

29

corresponding expansion in tourism but, to date, all terrestrial land is privately owned and available for development: no areas of coastal or inland woodland habitat have been designated for protection. The mangrove swamps remain the property of the Crown but, apart from Booby Pond, they too are unprotected.

Threats to species   In Little Cayman, the site of the breeding colonies of the Red-Footed Booby (around 3,500 pairs, the largest in the region) and the Magnificent Frigatebird is protected under international Treaty (Ramsar) and local legislation. However, new roads, increasing air traffic and a proposed new airport are major threats at the boundaries of the colony. If the disturbance becomes too great, the birds may move away. Regular monitoring is required to ensure that these two breeding species retain viable populations in this wetland.

An eradication programme is needed urgently to control feral animals. Packs of feral dogs hunt throughout the swamps in Grand Cayman, where they are major predators on waterfowl. Even more serious are the large number of feral cats throughout the three Islands threatening breeding Whistling-Ducks in the three Islands, the Booby and Frigatebird colonies in Little Cayman and nesting parrots in Grand Cayman and Cayman Brac.

Amendments to the Animals Law, 1976 protect most species from legal hunting. But the hunting season of the White-crowned Pigeon includes part of its peak breeding season; the closed season needs to be extended as, despite the seemingly large numbers in migration through the Cayman Islands, this species is classified as threatened throughout its limited range. In the absence of wardens, the Gun Club needs to encourage enforcement of the law against illegal hunting of protected species.

The expanded cage bird trade has led to over twenty species of exotics being bred successfully in captivity. To date four species of escaped cage birds, two doves and two parrots, have established feral breeding populations. The feral species pose a threat to the endemics as they will

30

compete for food and, in some cases, for breeding habitat. With small endangered populations, like the Cayman Brac parrot, competition could rapidly lead to extinction.

Conservation efforts   The National Trust for the Cayman Islands has initiated a Land Fund to purchase areas of land containing representative habitats. A major project is purchasing land at the Mountain to preserve the last large area of pristine woodland in Grand Cayman. The Trust, with the help of the Nature Conservancy-US, has acquired two areas of breeding habitat on the bluff on Cayman Brac for the endangered sub-species of Cayman Parrot. Also it has purchased land at the Mountain and, with the help of RARE, has opened a woodland trail. Another promising start has been made by the Governor's Fund purchasing for the Trust a few acres of supporting grassland and sedge around a freshwater pond at Newlands, Grand Cayman. This small, but very important, wetland is surrounded by houses and the support of residents sets an important precedent for conservation in the Cayman Islands.

The declaration of more protected bird areas (i.e habitats) is of paramount importance. Presently only the following have been given legal protection as Sanctuaries: Meagre Bay Pond and Colliers Pond, Grand Cayman and Booby Pond, Little Cayman. Owned by the National Trust, and protected under Trust law, are Governor's Pond and the Salina, Grand Cayman and two parrot reserves on the bluff, Cayman Brac.

There is now cautious optimism for Cayman's only breeding duck, the West Indian Whistling-Duck (*Dendrocygna arborea*), as the decline in numbers seems to have halted following a public awareness conservation drive. Local and international campaigns on behalf of the Cayman amazon parrot resulted in its removal from the list of game species, protection from harvesting for the pet trade and the protection of two breeding areas in Cayman Brac. As a result, population numbers of the endangered Cayman Brac sub-species have stabilized.

How to use the species accounts

All breeding birds, all regular migrants whether common or rare and all casual species are described in the text, as well as some very rare and exotic species included for ease of reference. The majority of vagrants and exotics are listed in Appendix 2.

Nomenclature Similar species appear under their Family name; each species has its English name in capitals on the left-hand side of the page, the local name in brackets and the scientific names of the genus and species in italics. The sequence follows the American Ornithologists' Union 1983 Check-list of North American Birds, 6th edition. The sub-specific names are from Bond (1956). The plate number in the text denotes the plate page number (in a square) in the central photographic portfolio, while an encircled number on the photograph after the species name denotes the text page.

Begin by making sure you are familiar with the topography of a bird from the drawings and other terms in the Glossary. Note your first impression of a new species and attempt to find the Family group to which it belongs. If a waterbird, is it a seabird, a heron or a shorebird? If a landbird, is it a bird of prey, one of the pigeons or a small passerine? Also note the habitat. Species are described under the following headings.

Field characters The average size is given in centimetres (cm) and inches (in) followed by a description of the plumages of the adult and immature bird. The diagnostic features are in italics. When observing an unknown species, the points to notice are the relative SIZE (heron or warbler) and the SHAPE of the body (fat, elongate, squat) especially in relation to bill and leg length, of the bill (curved, hooked, straight, long, thick), of the tail (square, forked, pointed), and of the wings in flight (long and pointed, short, rounded). Look at the overall COLOUR of the feathers and of the bare parts (legs, lore, bill); next note any distinctive markings of the head (the superciliary (eyebrow) stripe, eye-line, eye-ring), of the upperparts (wing-bars on folded wing, crown different to back, rump), of the underparts (throat, breast, abdomen, sides), and of the tail (spots, bars and bands, under

MANGROVE SWAMP AND POND

1

FRESHWATER POND:
GOVERNOR'S POND, NEWLANDS, GRAND CAYMAN

2

COASTAL HABITAT

3

WOODLAND ON BLUFF LIMESTONE,
GRAND CAYMAN

DRY BUSHLAND ON BLUFF LIMESTONE
EASTERN GRAND CAYMAN

5

PASTURE

9

URBAN/LITTORAL HABITAT BEHIND COASTAL IRONSHORE

7

THE BLUFF, CAYMAN BRAC,
OVERLOOKING NORTHERN COASTAL PLAIN

8

tail-coverts); note any distinctive wing markings in flight (wing stripes are often diagnostic in shorebirds, as is speculum colour in ducks).

Plumage is described for breeding and non-breeding stages, and in some cases for juvenile and immature plumages. The field characters of some species are given in detail: these are either endemic sub-species, whose plumage descriptions are usually only otherwise available in ornithological publications, or migrant shorebirds and warblers which are not illustrated. Feathers become worn and faded before they are moulted and replaced each year. Feather wear or a moult stage can make identification difficult especially in shorebirds in winter; conversely the bright new feathers of a juvenile wader can make it look very different from the adult. Much practice is needed to separate different migrant warblers in non-breeding and immature plumages.

Range   The breeding range is first, followed, after a semi-colon, by the non-breeding range if the species is partially or completely migratory. For cosmopolitan species distribution outside the Americas may be mentioned. This biogeographic information explains most of the migration patterns through the Cayman Islands, for example, many of the very rare migrants only occur here due to the position of the Islands at the extreme western end of the Caribbean chain which, apart from western Cuba, is the closest landfall to Central America.

Cayman habitat   The preferred areas where the bird breeds and forages within the Islands. Named sites have been included if they are regular breeding areas or are species specific. As an aid to identification the Island habitats have been classified into four types, each with a list of associated common bird species. It is worth remembering that as an adaptation to life in small islands, many species have a wide habitat distribution occurring almost everywhere, but the **preferred** habitats are the most likely areas for the species to occur. See Maps in Appendix 3.

1. Wetlands: mangrove swamps and associated saline lagoons and ponds, secondary swamp;

flooded marl pits (quarries); grassland freshwater ponds, brackish sedge and cat-tail (*Typha* sp.) swamps [Plates 1, 2]. Four species make up the marine mangrove ecosystem: Red Mangrove (*Rhizophora mangle*), Black Mangrove (*Avicennia germinans*), White Mangrove (*Laguncularia racemosa*) and Buttonwood (*Conocarpus erectus*); the communities occur in mixed and single species stands and can tolerate a wide variation in salinity. The coastal Red Mangrove, known as an "island-builder", gradually claims new land from the sea and, with Black Mangrove, forms a coastal fringe round the extensive North Sound, Grand Cayman. The shallow lagoons and ponds lying behind the coastal beach ridges are fringed with differing proportions of the four species. The salinity of the water varies from hyper-saline in the dry season, owing to percolation through the substrate from the sea, to brackish, due to run-off following heavy rains. Much of the mangrove floor is flooded in June and from August to December, providing a safe refuge and rich feeding ground for the arriving migrant waterbirds and warblers. Monospecific Buttonwood forms inland swamps in depressions in the Bluff limestone in Grand Cayman. Secondary swamp, i.e. swamp which has been cleared and is regenerating, and urban areas being built on wetlands are the preferred habitat of many migrants.

Grassy freshwater ponds and brackish *Typha* sp. and sedge swamps only occur to any significant extent in Grand Cayman.

For the best birding sites see text accompanying Map 1. Excellent swamp maps, prepared by the Mosquito Research and Control Unit (MRCU) and available from the Lands and Survey Department, are recommended for serious wetland birdwatchers. The maps show the area and species distribution of the mangrove, the lagoons and ponds in the three Islands. In Grand Cayman only, they show the system of MRCU dyke roads, single tracks bordered by canals connected to the North Sound. However many of the dyke roads and much of the mangrove west of Savannah have been filled for development; those remaining are an excellent means to access the swamps on foot.

This is the preferred habitat for the Pied-billed Grebe,

herons, egrets, the Least Bittern and the Purple Gallinule in freshwater and sedge ponds, ibises and the spoonbill, ducks, raptors, rails, plovers, sandpipers, the stilt, some gulls and terns, pigeons and doves, the parrot in Grand Cayman, the kingfisher, woodpeckers in Grand Cayman, the Loggerhead Kingbird, vireos, resident and migrant warblers, the bananaquit, the bullfinch in Grand Cayman, and the grackle in Grand Cayman and Little Cayman. Frigatebirds and boobies breed in this habitat in Little Cayman only.

2. Coastal habitat, including the fringing reefs, the sea edge, the shore, the littoral woodland or bushland behind the shore, and the marine bluffs (cliffs) [Plates 3, 7]. The shore is either sandy beach or Ironshore. In areas unaltered by man, the littoral vegetation is woodland or bushland, often monospecific Sea-grape (*Coccoloba uvifera*); on exposed shores the bushland closest to the sea consists of low shrubs. Under man's influence, this belt also includes Australian Pine (*Casuarina equisetifola*), Coconut Palm (*Cocos nucifera*), Almond (*Terminalia catappa*) and Red Birch (*Bursera simaruba)*. It becomes an urban/littoral area when it describes gardens along the shore in altered littoral woodland, see 4. below.

This is the preferred habitat for tropicbirds and the Brown Booby on the marine bluffs of Cayman Brac and Grand Cayman, frigatebirds, cormorants, herons and egrets, plovers and sandpipers, gulls and terns, the Osprey, pigeons and doves, the parrot in Grand Cayman and Cayman Brac, the kingfisher, woodpeckers, cuckoos, nighthawks, owls, flycatchers, swallows, migrant vireos and warblers, migrant tanagers and grosbeaks and buntings, the grassquit, and the grackle in Grand Cayman and Little Cayman.

3. Woodland and bushland associated with Bluff Formation rock [Plates 4, 5]. The endemic terrestrial vegetation which grows precariously on the exposed Bluff Formation is the major habitat for endemic landbirds. Once extensive hardwood forests covered the drier eastern regions of Grand Cayman and the bluff of Cayman Brac. By the beginning of this century almost all the mature trees had been felled. The present vegetation is secondary woodland (trees over 10 metres) and bushland (trees and shrubs under 10 metres) and may include (not all species are present on the three Islands) Mahogany, Ironwood, Cedar and Wild Fig, Royal Palms, the predominant Red Birch, Thatch Palms, Popnut, Almond, Manchineel, Logwood (introduced in the 18th century into Grand Cayman only, it occurs as mono-specific secondary woodland, or a mixed community with Buttonwood), Wild Cinnamon, Cabbage Tree, Wild Sapo-dilla, Whitewood, Fiddlewood, Wild Cherry, Balsam, Straw-berry Tree, Pepper Cinnamon, Smokewood, Cherry and Poison Tree, all mixed with vines, bromeliads, orchids, climbing cacti and maidenplum (see Bibliography: The Flora of the Cayman Islands). Depressions in the limestone hold freshwater and are associated with monospecific Buttonwood swamps in eastern Grand Cayman. The eastern bluffs in the three Islands, with lower rainfall and increased wind ex-posure, have low dry bushland habitat where Thatch Palms (*Thrinax* sp.), Agave and Wild Jasmine (*Plumeria* sp.) predominate.

This is the preferred habitat for some pigeons and doves, parrots in Grand Cayman and Cayman Brac, woodpeckers, flycatchers, the thrush in Cayman Brac, vireos, warblers, tanagers and buntings.

4. Habitats altered by man: urban areas including gardens, urban/littoral areas, scrub, roadsides, pas-ture, plantations, dry marl pits and spoil banks [Plates 6, 7]. Urban areas along the coastal littoral are one of the best places to see migrant birds in the Islands. Increased land clearing for urban development and the cultivation of fruit trees has led to increased populations of many of the most frequently seen species: the Cattle Egret, White-winged Dove, ani, Gray Kingbird, mockingbirds and grassquits. Also seen are herons and egrets, terns, swallows, nighthawks, parrots in Grand Cayman and Cayman Brac, migrant war-blers and vireos, and bananaquits.

Habits Diagnostic behaviour in habitat, feeding methods, flight characteristics. The breeding season is often protracted in the tropics and may extend throughout the year. Breeding behaviour includes courtship, the time when eggs and young are attended by parents, nest type and height from the ground, and clutch size. Song and calls are an excellent diagnostic means of identifying endemic landbirds and migrant shorebirds; many migrant landbirds are silent in passage though some of the winter warblers sing in spring.

Status Estimate of abundance; whether a bird is breeding as a resident or summer visitor, or is a winter migrant, a passage migrant or a casual visitor; in which of the Cayman Islands the bird occurs; estimate of frequency. The only sub-specific names given are those of the 17 endemics.

Abundance. The approximate number of birds expected to be seen in preferred habitats, in appropriate seasons, is estimated as follows:

Abundant	over 60 birds in a day.
Very common	seen in large numbers on all birding expeditions, 30+birds/day.
Common	10 to 30 birds/day.
Locally common	normally uncommon or rare migrant occasionally seen for short periods in considerable numbers.
Fairly common	2 to 10 birds/day.
Uncommon	0 to 2 birds/day.
Rare	0 to 4 sightings per season.
Very rare	1 to 10 sightings since 1886 (very rare birds differ from vagrants as they include the Cayman Islands within their non-breeding range, Appendix 2).

Breeding birds are classified as follows:
Breeding resident: breeding confirmed, present throughout the year.
Summer breeding visitor: breeding confirmed, present only part of the year.
Intermittent breeder: breeding not recorded each year.
Previously reported as breeding: no records since 1975.

Residents are classified as present throughout the year, breeding not proved.

Migrants are classified as follows:

Winter visitors: long-stay non-breeding migrants, chiefly from November to February with a few present throughout the year.

Passage migrants: non-breeding, usually in fall and spring, though may occur in any season as short-stay visitors. Between August and November the majority are en route to their wintering grounds in Central and South America; between March to May they are returning to North America to breed.

Casual: not regular visitors; call here occasionally in no special season; the Cayman Islands lie within their non-breeding range.

Vagrant: accidental visitors, not expected to occur (Appendix 2).

GLOSSARY

Barred	feather pattern of transverse stripes.
Breeding plumage	feathers worn just before, during and for varying periods after nesting.
Buff	pale whitish brown.
Call	short vocalization, characteristic of each species.
Colour morph	colour phase within a species.
Cosmopolitan	worldwide.
Crepuscular	active in dim light, dawn and dusk.
Distal	furthest from the body.
Diurnal	active by day.
Eclipse	post-nuptial plumage stage, often refers to ducks and geese.
Ecosystem	natural environment: plants, animals, birds, the land or water.
Endemic	confined to one region.
Extirpated	extinct in some parts of its range.
Extinct	worldwide loss of a species.
Feral	introduced species living in the wild.
Forage	search for food.
Greater Antilles	Northern West Indies, Cuba to the Virgin Islands.
Gular sac	see throat pouch.
Immature	intermediate plumage between juvenile and adult.
Introduced	brought by man; may become feral breeder.
Juvenile	first feather covering, replacing the down of the chick.
Mask	contrasting band across face, including the eyes.
Pelagic	birds which wander the oceans.
Primaries	long flight feathers on outermost part of wing.
Rump	area between back and tail, may describe area of contrasting colour including lower back and upper tail-coverts.

Secondaries	flight feathers on innermost part of wing.
Song	series of vocalized phrases, usually by the male in the breeding season.
Stripe	longitudinal stripes.
Sub-species	recognizably different geographical form of a species.
Throat pouch	gular sac; area of bare skin on throat; may inflate.
Underparts	ventral surface; chin, throat, breast, abdomen, sides, and undertail.
Upperparts	dorsal surface; crown, nape, back, rump and uppertail; can include wings if same colour.
Urban/littoral	habitat altered by man, gardens in the vegetation behind the shore.
West Indies	Greater and Lesser Antilles and the Bahamas.
Wing-bar	coloured stripe along the wing coverts.
Wing-coverts	small feathers, arranged in rows, covering the upper and lower surfaces of the wing.

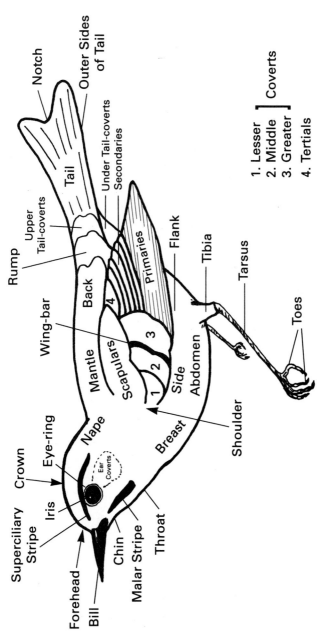

TOPOGRAPHY OF A BIRD

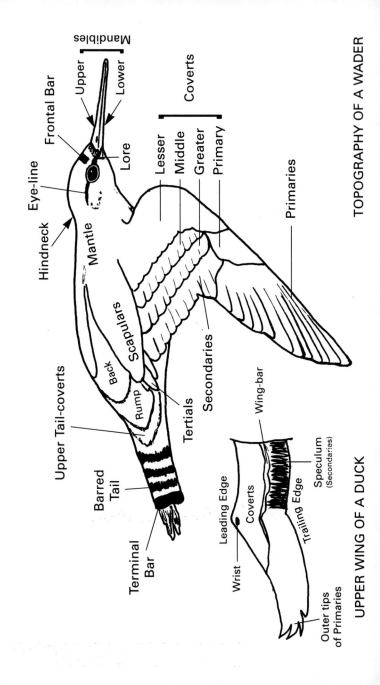

TOPOGRAPHY OF A WADER

UPPER WING OF A DUCK

Mandibles
Upper
Lower
Frontal Bar
Lore
Eye-line
Hindneck
Mantle
Scapulars
Back
Rump
Upper Tail-coverts
Barred Tail
Terminal Bar
Tertials
Secondaries
Lesser
Middle
Greater
Primary
Coverts
Primaries

Wrist
Leading Edge
Coverts
Wing-bar
Trailing Edge
Speculum (Secondaries)
Outer tips of Primaries

SPECIES
ACCOUNTS

FAMILY PODICIPEDIDAE: GREBES. Only one species, a breeding resident, is represented. Small, shy duck-like divers reluctant to fly, usually submerge or dive when alarmed.

PIED-BILLED GREBE (Diver; Diving Dapper)
Podilymbus podiceps   **Plate 9**

Field characters. 33cm:12in A small stocky diver; large flattened head; thick whitish chicken-like bill; white eye-ring; *white fluffy under tail-coverts* and abdomen; reduced tail; dark legs placed far back for strong swimming. Sexes alike, though male is larger. Breeding: *black sub-terminal band around bill; black chin and throat patch;* blackish crown and nape; brownish grey back and wings; sides of face and neck are pale greyish buff in Cayman birds; neck and breast brownish grey; sides barred whitish and greyish brown. Non-breeding adult and immature: darker face; whitish throat; brown bill appears smaller; neck, breast and flanks barred chestnut grey; back blackish grey; throat patch and ring around bill reduced in adult, absent in immature. Juvenile: striped head and neck, red face skin. Breeding season extends throughout the year so complete non-breeding plumage is seldom seen.

Range. Cayman Islands, West Indies, North America to northern South America.

Cayman habitat. Mangrove-fringed lagoons and ponds; most freshwater ponds and flooded marl pits (quarries), Grand Cayman.

Habits. Singles or pairs usual; rafts (groups) on Meagre Bay/Pease Bay Ponds, Grand Cayman and on Tarpon Lake, Little Cayman. An extremely shy bird, sinking silently or diving and swimming under water when alarmed. Controls buoyancy by expelling air, usually floats low in the water or with only the head and neck showing; only floats high when unafraid. Breeds in all seasons, clutch 3–8, in a mud raft nest; pretty striped chicks are often carried on their parents' backs.

Calls: long harsh series *cac-cac-cac-wo-wo-kwo-kwo-caa-caa*, becoming longer and descending; also a single low *kuk* from the female to young.

Status. Common breeding resident, Grand Cayman and fairly common, Little Cayman; an uncommon migrant, Cayman Brac, where there are no recent breeding records.

FAMILY PHAETHONTIDAE: TROPICBIRDS. Three species occur in the world; one species is a summer breeding visitor in the Islands; sexes alike.

WHITE-TAILED TROPICBIRD (Boatswain bird)
Phaethon lepturus   **Plates 10, 11**

Field characters. 40cm:16in (plus 40 cm:16in tail streamers). A shining white tern-like bird. Adult: black patch on outer primaries; *black diagonal band along wing coverts;* black streak through eye; orange decurved bill; pointed tail with two *elongated central tail streamers;* black feet. Immature: back barred blackish and white; yellow bill; pointed tail with streamers absent; smaller than adult.

Range. Cayman Islands. Cosmopolitan; over tropical oceans.

Cayman habitat. Main colony breeds from Stake Bay to Spot Bay along the north-east face of the bluff, Cayman Brac; small colony breeds on the bluff between Spotts and Pedro, Grand Cayman. Foraging birds in coastal waters.

Habits. Small groups perform aerobatics, calling to each other, *ke-ke-ke*, as they swoop and soar displaying beautiful plumage; also a rapid wingbeat flight. Like boobies, they dive to catch fish and squid, frequently chased and robbed by Frigatebirds on their return to land. Nest in colonies, clutch of 1, in crevices in the cliff face, breeding April-July.

Status. Summer breeding visitor, January to September; very common, Cayman Brac; uncommon, Grand Cayman.

FAMILY SULIDAE: BOOBIES. Pelagic seabirds which dive for prey and have an elaborate courtship display. Two species are resident, breeding in Little Cayman and Cayman Brac; sexes alike; adult plumage is assumed after three years.

BROWN BOOBY (Booby)   *Sula leucogaster*
Plate 12

Field characters. 71cm:28in Adult: dark chocolate brown plumage apart from sharply defined *white lower breast to under tail- and under wing-coverts;* long neck; pointed tail; yellowish bill bluish distally; yellowish feet and legs. Breeding: blackish spot in front of the eye; bill yellow, whitish pink distally; facial skin and gular sac yellow. Immature: *entirely brown,* paler on the abdomen and under wing-coverts; bluish grey face and dark bill.

Range. Cayman Islands. Cosmopolitan; over tropical oceans.

Cayman habitat. Resident and breeding from the extreme north-eastern bluff to along the south facing bluff, Cayman Brac; occasional sightings in coastal waters off Grand Cayman and Little Cayman.

Habits. Fly singly, or in groups in skeins, flapping and gliding with neck outstretched, often close to water's surface. Dive for fish, often pursued by Frigatebirds; return each night to roost unless food is scarce, when they remain out at sea. Breeding from October to June; one white egg is laid on the rocks of the bluff cliffs; the large fluffy chick takes 16 to 18 weeks to fledge.

Status. Fairly common breeding resident, Cayman Brac. (**Note.** A pair of Masked Boobies has remained with this colony since 1985; see Appendix 2.)

RED-FOOTED BOOBY (Booby)   *Sula sula*
Plate 13, 14

Field characters. 71cm:28in Adults show dimorphic (two colour) phases in the Cayman Islands. All: long narrow wings;

pink at base of bill; *white tail, rump, upper back and under tail-coverts;* diagnostic *red feet. Ten per cent of the colony are white morphs with blackish brown primaries, secondaries and carpel patch on the under wing;* in breeding plumage a golden wash develops on crown. *Ninety per cent are brown morphs, with brown head, mantle, abdomen and darker wings and breast;* in breeding plumage head and neck become silvery brown. Breeding, both morphs: the mask becomes brightly coloured, facial skin and around the eye pale turquoise blue; pink around the base of the mandibles and along the bluish bill becomes brighter; black line delimits the face skin forming a long V under the lower mandible. Immature: *entirely brown;* blackish bill; blue facial skin; olive to yellow feet.

Range. Cayman Islands. Cosmopolitan; throughout tropical oceans.

Cayman habitat. Permanent breeding and roosting colony, approximately 3,500 pairs, is associated with a Magnificent Frigatebird colony in Little Cayman; nests in the mangrove fringe and the woodland behind on the landward side of Booby Pond, an area called the Rookery. Forages off the western shore of Cayman Brac and, rarely, in Grand Cayman waters.

Habits. Most adults and many immatures fly out to sea at dawn and spend the day diving for fish. Returning at dusk, they are attacked by waiting Frigatebirds; spectacular avian battles result as the boobies are chased across the sky in an effort to make them disgorge their crop contents. One of two species of Booby to nest in trees; breeding from November to June; clutch of 1, in a rough nest platform, November to late December. The large white fluffy chick sits patiently for 14–16 weeks; the majority fledge by April. When food is scarce parents only return to the nest every 4 to 5 days.

Status. Very common breeding resident, Little Cayman.

FAMILY PELECANIDAE: PELICANS. Large, heavy birds with distinctive bills and throat pouches; two species occur in the region, only one species is a regular visitor.

BROWN PELICAN   *Pelecanus occidentalis*

Field characters. 122 cm:48 in Appears dark brown in flight, with black primaries and a flap and glide flight; *large pouched bill.* Adult non-breeding: white crown and neck; rest of plumage brown. Breeding: yellow crown and chest patch; white neck stripe; *chestnut nape* and abdomen; silvery sheen on back and closed wing. Immature: whitish brown with greyish white underparts.

Range. West Indies, coasts of tropical and sub-tropical North to South America.

Cayman habitat. Singles or small groups, often after storms, close inshore including marine sounds; over-winter in mangrove-fringed lagoons.

Status. Uncommon, casual in the three Islands, usually as short-stay visitors though birds, usually immatures, occasionally over-winter.

FAMILY PHALACROCORACIDAE: CORMORANTS.

DOUBLE-CRESTED CORMORANT   *Phalacrocorax auritus*

Field characters. 84cm:33 in Adult: large iridescent black bird; slender black hooked bill; bright *orange facial skin and throat pouch;* green eye; wings show grey in flight. Immature: brownish upperparts; buffy neck and breast. Neck has a kink in flight.

Range. Cuba, the Bahamas, North America.

Cayman habitat. Coastal; mangrove lagoons.

Status. Rare, casual in the three Islands after winter storms; single birds, usually immature, occasionally over-winter.
(**Note.** The Olivaceous Cormorant (*Phalacrocorax olivaceus*) may be expected to occur as a vagrant; it breeds in Cuba and the Bahamas).

FAMILY ANHINGIDAE: DARTERS.
Diving birds, capable of remaining underwater for extended periods.

ANHINGA   *Anhinga anhinga*

Field characters. 86cm:34in Long slim neck bent in a G; long *straight serrated bill* unlike hooked bill of cormorant; long tail. Male: glossy black; *silver feathers on wing coverts and scapulars.* Female: *pale brown head, neck and breast.* Immature: brownish.

Range. Cuba, coasts of tropical and sub-tropical North to South Americas.

Cayman habitat. Coastal, including mangrove in marine sounds.

Habits. Swims with only head and neck showing; perches in trees often with wings held open to dry the feathers or reduce body temperature.

Status. Rare, casual, most frequent in Little Cayman and Cayman Brac following winter storms; single birds occasionally over-winter.

FAMILY FREGATIDAE: FRIGATEBIRDS.
Large, very light aerial birds which spend the day on the wing. Breed in colonies often associated with Boobies or other colonial sea-birds. One species is represented in the Islands.

MAGNIFICENT FRIGATEBIRD (Man O' War)
Fregata magnificens   **Plates 15, 16, 17**

Field characters. 102cm:40in Very large seabird. In flight, *long, narrow, scimitar-like, wings;* black plumage with violet bronze sheen; forked tail, appears pointed when folded; long, bluish white hooked bill. It takes five years to reach maturity; the plumages are as follows:

Adult male: *entirely glossy black; red extendable gular sac in the breeding season.*

Adult female: plumage entirely blackish brown with shiny bronze diagonal across wings, except for *white breast and flanks* and small red feet; larger than male.

Immatures: first and second year, *head and breast white,* remainder of plumage brownish black. During the third and fourth years white plumage is gradually replaced to form the adult pattern.

Range. Cayman Islands, West Indies and the coasts of the tropical Americas.

Cayman habitat. Soars over the Islands' coasts and reefs. A large breeding colony, associated with the Red-footed Booby, is located at the edge of the mangrove on a lagoon, Booby Pond, Little Cayman; non-breeding birds roost in trees on the south shore, Little Cayman and in mangrove on Man O' War Cay, Snug Harbour, Grand Cayman; coastal, Cayman Brac.

Habits. Fly with wings bent in shallow M. Mostly remain on the wing during the day, except in breeding season. Frequently seen in groups in George Town Harbour, Grand Cayman, wheeling and diving as fisherman clean fish; also perch on fishing boats at sea. The aerial mastery is allowed by an extremely low wing loading: a wingspan of 2.5m and a total body weight of around 1–2 kg. In Cayman Brac and Little Cayman the Frigatebirds partly depend on robbing the Brown and Red-footed Boobies of their day's catch; they also eat fish, squid and baby turtles. Breeding: from late November to May, the males fly with scarlet gular sacs inflated; on the nest they display these sacs by holding their bill pointed upwards, raising the mantle of elongated feathers while making a hollow drumming sound. Laying is synchronous in

January, clutch of one, most hatch during February. The chick, white with dark down feathers on the back, is fed and brooded by both parents for 12 to 14 weeks, then by the female until fledged at about six months. In April the majority of males leave the colony for approximately six months.

Status. Very common breeding resident, Little Cayman. Fairly common, non-breeding, Grand Cayman and Cayman Brac.

FAMILY ARDEIDAE: HERONS. Eleven species are represented; six are breeding residents. The very rare American Bittern is included here for ease of comparison. Great size variation; stabbing bills and the neck folded back into shoulders in flight characterize these waterbirds; sexes alike.

AMERICAN BITTERN   *Botaurus lentiginosus*

Field characters. 60cm:25in Medium sized heron; upperparts brown with light and darker spots, a beautiful and subtle mingling of tones; creamy throat continuing to breast with brown streaks; light brown streaked underparts; *black lines from lower mandible down sides of throat;* legs and bill yellowish brown. Flight similar to Night-Herons, showing blackish primaries and secondaries.

Range. North America; winters in the breeding range, Mexico and the Greater Antilles.

Cayman habitat. Secondary swamp; grassland close to water.

Habits. Freezes like a Least Bittern when alarmed; walks in a deliberate manner with shoulders hunched.

Status. Very rare in passage in the three Islands, mainly

September to March; one bird spent part of the winter in Little Cayman, February to March 1984.

LEAST BITTERN   *Ixobrychus exilis*

Field characters. 30cm:12in A diminutive heron; adults show diagnostic *yellowish buff patch on lesser wing-coverts, bordered by chestnut upper coverts and inner secondaries.* Male: *crown and upperparts greenish black;* sides of face and hindneck brownish to chestnut; underparts whitish streaked with cinnamon or buff; blackish patch at the point of the 'shoulder'; bill yellow, dark on upper mandible; legs and feet yellowish black. Female: paler; *crown and upperparts dark chocolate brown;* striped brown throat; resembles a young Green Heron but wing patches diagnostic. Immature: buffy overall; upperparts brownish edged with buff; dusky streaks on wing coverts; dusky streaking on buffy throat and breast.

Range. Greater Antilles, North America to South America; North American birds winter to the Greater Antilles, Central and South America.

Cayman habitat. Mainly freshwater and brackish cat-tail (*Typha* sp.) swamps including Governor's Pond, Newlands; occasionally in mangrove; Grand Cayman only.

Habits. Very secretive, heard more often than seen; calls: soft *cu-cu-cu-cu* among the reeds at dawn and dusk, low hard alarm *ke-ke-ke* and a loud cackling. Clings unto cat-tails, when flushed it flies a short distance and drops back into the reeds; also walks rail-like among grass roots at the edge of ponds. Like the American Bittern it remains immobile with bill pointing vertically when startled.

Status. Uncommon to fairly common resident and winter visitor, Grand Cayman; breeding not confirmed, young immatures regular but no definite nesting records. No records from Cayman Brac or Little Cayman, possibly due to lack of suitable habitat.

GREAT BLUE HERON   *Ardea herodias*

Field characters. 120cm:48in Our largest heron; heavily built with long thick neck and bill. Adult: predominantly grey in the field; *white head with black lateral stripes forming a crest; face and throat white;* grey upperparts; blackish streaks on neck to breast; black shoulders; abdomen blackish with cinnamon streaks; chestnut thighs; blackish olive legs; bill yellowish to bright yellow in breeding plumage. In flight shows black primaries and secondaries. Immature: brownish grey; dark crown.

Range. West Indies, North to South America. Migrants to the Cayman Islands probably come from North America.

Cayman habitat. Lagoons and ponds; shores, marine sounds and fringing reefs; a roost on mangrove cay, Snug Harbour, Grand Cayman; occasionally on the bluff, Cayman Brac.

Habits. Stands immobile when awaiting fish, frogs and small mammals, stabbing with powerful bill; call: *qu-aark* when alarmed; flies with slow majestic wingbeats. Usually solitary by day except in migration or in feeding aggregates and roosts with other herons.

Status. Uncommon winter visitor and fairly common passage migrant in the three Islands, mainly August to May, though records for all months.

(**Note.** The white morph of this species (not yet recorded here) resembles the Great Egret but is larger and heavier with *yellow legs*).

GREAT EGRET   *Casmerodius albus*

Field characters. 95cm:38in Very large slim heron. Entirely white plumage; *long yellow bill; black legs and feet.* Breeding: green lores; long trailing dorsal plumes.

Range. West Indies, North to South America. Cosmopolitan.

Cayman habitat. Mangrove lagoons and swamps; shores and fringing reefs; freshwater ponds, Grand Cayman.

Habits. Usually solitary, though small groups occur in feeding aggregates and roosts with other herons; when foraging, freezes with body bent forwards and head and neck extended; graceful flight.

Status. Fairly common winter visitor and passage migrant, Grand Cayman and Little Cayman; fairly common in passage and a few over-winter, Cayman Brac; mainly August to May though records for all months.

SNOWY EGRET (White gauldin)   *Egretta thula*
    Plate 18

Field characters. 63cm:25in Adult: entirely white plumage, *entirely black bill and legs; yellow feet; yellow lores*; beautiful curved plumes on neck, breast and back in breeding season. Immature: smaller; black bill may show paler at base; yellow lores; black stripe down *front of yellowish legs;* yellowish feet.

Range. Cayman Islands, West Indies, North America to South America.

Cayman habitat. Throughout the wetlands, including swamps, lagoons, ponds; the Ironshore; grassy freshwater ponds, Grand Cayman. Large (1,000 pairs plus) permanent breeding colony in the mangrove fringing North Sound, Grand Cayman; breeds intermittently along with Red-footed Boobies and other herons at the back of Booby Pond, Little Cayman. Roosts with other herons at Meagre Bay Pond, Grand Cayman and westerly ponds, Cayman Brac.

Habits. Seen singly or in flocks up to several hundred adults and immatures in feeding aggregates with other herons, waders and stilts on lagoons and ponds. Shows great variety of feeding techniques including hovering, flying over water surface dipping for food, dashing to and fro in shallow water with wings partially open, and foot stirring the mud to dislodge prey. Flies between the three Islands. Calls: croaking and loud squawks between magnificently plumaged breeding adults. Breeding, December-April; small, roughly made nests, 4–10 metres elevation in trees, clutch 3–4, fledge in 4 to 5 weeks.

Status. Common to abundant breeding resident, Grand Cayman; intermittent breeder, Little Cayman, common to very common in winter becoming scarce during summer, droughts or non-breeding years. Fairly common resident, non-breeding, Cayman Brac, though large flocks of several hundred occur in post-breeding dispersals.

LITTLE BLUE HERON (Blue gauldin) *Egretta caerulea* Plates 19, 20

Field characters. 69cm:27in Medium-sized, slender heron. Adult: slate blue body; head and neck purple grey; *bluish bill with black tip, bluish grey lores; legs pale olive.* First year birds are white but show *greyish primaries* in flight; *grey lores, bill chalky blue; legs greenish.* (Note: Snowy Egret adults show white primaries; yellow lores; black bill and legs; yellow feet.) Immature changing to adult plumage, known as a calico, is mottled with blue grey into the second year.

Range. Cayman Islands, West Indies, eastern United States to South America.

Cayman habitat. Mangrove swamps, lagoons and small ponds; the Ironshore and reef-protected shores; brackish and freshwater ponds, Grand Cayman. Breeding habitat as for Snowy Egret.

Habits. Mainly solitary, though groups of adults and immatures occur at the edge of feeding aggregates. Breeds intermittently with other herons (nest shape and height are similar); clutch 2, incubate for about 21 days. Often flies for considerable distances with neck outstretched, resembling a Glossy Ibis.

Status. Fairly common to common resident, and intermittent and uncommon breeding species, Grand Cayman and Little Cayman; non-breeding resident, Cayman Brac. Adults predominate in winter, immatures in summer as the population is partially migratory.

TRICOLORED HERON (Grey gauldin) *Egretta tricolor*
Plates 21, 22

Field characters. 65cm:26in Adult: predominantly blue grey; long thin neck with a grey and white band from throat to breast; *white throat, abdomen, sides, rump and under wing-coverts;* bill yellowish with black tip; lores yellow; legs olive to yellow. Breeding: bright blue replaces yellow on the bill; legs red; *long pale chestnut plumes on the crown and back.* Immature: grey mostly replaced by chestnut on neck, back and wing coverts.

Range. Cayman Islands, Greater Antilles and the Bahamas, United States, Central to South America.

Cayman habitat. All wetland habitats. Breeds along with Snowy Egrets in mangrove at the edge of North Sound, Grand Cayman, and intermittently in woodland, Little Cayman.

Habits. Large groups in feeding aggregates with other herons in the early morning, otherwise usually solitary. Flies for short distances with neck outstretched like an ibis, giving a complaining croaking call. Nest similar to Snowy Egret; clutch 3–4; chicks have dark grey on wings and back, unlike other species which are entirely white. Juveniles climb into the fine branches above the nest at about 19 to 23 days and fly in 4 to 6 weeks.

Status. Very common breeding resident, Grand Cayman and, intermittently, Little Cayman (scarce in summer); fairly common resident, non-breeding, Cayman Brac.

REDDISH EGRET   *Egretta rufescens*

Field characters. 75cm: 29in Dimorphic, white and dark morphs; both with *bicoloured bill flesh-pink at the base, black distally;* grey pink lores, blackish legs and feet. Breeding: bill brighter; long plumes on scapulars extend over tail; plumes on head and neck appear shaggy; legs blue. White morph: entirely white. Dark morph: dark grey body, dull brownish grey head and neck becoming reddish when breeding. Immature, both morphs: *bill blackish, not bicoloured, grey lores;* dark morph is greyish with greyish brown on head, neck and wing patches; white morph resembles a Snowy Egret but is larger, heavier with a longer neck, *dark feet* and a stouter bill.

Range. Greater Antilles, Bahamas, southern United States, Mexico. Casual elsewhere in the West Indies.

Cayman habitat. Mangrove lagoons; shores.

Habits. Feeding behaviour is diagnostic: dashes around with neck extended and wings raised, often appears to dance, turning and twisting.

Status. First recorded in 1983; uncommon winter visitor and casual in all months in the three Islands; mainly immatures in both phases.

CATTLE EGRET (Cattle gauldin)   *Bubulcus ibis*
   Plates 23, 24

Field characters. 56cm:22in *Stocky, short-necked white egret; short yellow bill;* black to olive legs. Breeding: *crown, neck, breast and back become buffy orange;* eyes and bill become orange red; legs and feet range from yellow orange to red.

Range. Cayman Islands, West Indies and the Americas. Africa, becoming cosmopolitan.

Cayman habitat. Shores; disturbed habitat including grassland. Breeds in woodland with other herons, Little Cayman, and on the bluff, Cayman Brac. Roosts in mangrove, North Sound, Grand Cayman.

Habits. Terrestrial. Often associated with cattle in pasture.

Status. First recorded in the Islands in 1957 (Bond). Common winter and passage migrant and fairly common resident in the Islands. Breeds intermittently, Cayman Brac and Little Cayman; breeding is suspected, but not confirmed, Grand Cayman.

GREEN HERON (Mary Perk)   *Butorides virescens*
Plate 25

Field characters. 43cm:17in Short-legged small heron showing great colour and size variation. Adult: dark steely blue crown and back; *dark petrol blue wings with pale edging* to feathers, wings broad and rounded showing dark primaries in flight; *sides and back of neck chestnut* (varies from light to dark), whitish throat with brown bar along mandible; bill has upper mandible black, lower mandible yellow to olive; breast streaked white and mid-brown; sides greyish brown; abdomen olive; short tail; legs and feet vary from olive to bright orange in breeding birds. Immature: smaller and paler; chestnut replaced by brown streaks on neck; back and crown striped light and dark brown. A dark rufous adult phase is also seen.

Range. Cayman Islands, West Indies, central and eastern United States, Central America to Panama.

Cayman habitat. All wetland habitats including the Ironshore. Freshwater ponds; MRCU canals, Grand Cayman.

Habits. Solitary. Stalks prey along mangrove roots or pond edges, freezing except for *flickering tail*. Calls: loud raucous *k-yew* when alarmed, *raises crest* and flies to cover, maintains a warning series, *kek-kek-kek*. Roosts with neck folded, appearing very short and unheronlike. Nests on or near the ground in mangrove and around grassy ponds, clutch of 3, mainly March to August.

Status. Common breeding resident, Grand Cayman; fairly common to uncommon breeding resident, Little Cayman and Cayman Brac (dependent on water levels); also a winter and passage migrant from North America.

BLACK-CROWNED NIGHT-HERON *Nycticorax nycticorax*

Field characters. 62cm:24in Thick-set heron. Adult: *black crown and back;* grey wings, tail and sides of neck; whitish face, throat and underparts; red eyes; black bill; yellowish legs. Juvenile: as Yellow-crowned Night-Heron except bigger spots on back. Immature: upperparts and crown brownish, spotting reduced becoming absent, underparts pale becoming whitish. All: shorter yellowish to olive legs, *only the toes project behind the tail in flight;* narrower longer bill than the Yellow-crowned Night-Heron.

Range. West Indies, North, Central and South America. Africa and Eurasia.

Cayman habitat. Lagoon and pond edges, secondary and Buttonwood swamps; cat-tail or sedge ponds in open country; marl pit edges; throughout Grand Cayman.

Habits. Crepuscular and nocturnal; shy; roosts hunched with head on shoulders during the day. Flight call: a far-carrying *wark.*

Status. Uncommon winter visitor, Grand Cayman, August to May; no records, Cayman Brac or Little Cayman.

YELLOW-CROWNED NIGHT-HERON (Crab-catcher) *Nyctanassa violacea* **Plates 26, 27**

Field characters. 63cm:25in Stocky, medium-sized pale grey heron. Adult: diagnostic *horizontal black and white face pattern;* white crown becomes yellow with long white plumes in breeding season; neck and underparts pale grey; back and wings black with pale grey edges to feathers; short heavy black bill; yellow legs; orange red eyes. Juvenile: brownish grey with pale spots on back and wings; head and underparts are streaked whitish and olive. Immature: darker than Black-crowned Night Heron; centre crown and upperparts brownish slate with buff edges to feathers, spotting faint but mostly absent; underparts brownish buff, buffy posteriorly. In flight all show pronounced folded neck; yellowish *feet and lower legs project beyond tail* unlike the Black-crowned Night-Heron.

Range. Cayman Islands, West Indies, eastern United States to coastal Peru and Brazil.

Cayman habitat. Breeding in mangrove, Grand Cayman and Little Cayman; in woodland on the bluff, Cayman Brac. Forages on lagoon and pond edges, secondary swamp; sand beaches; roads.

Habits. Upright stance; despite its name, seen during the day as well as at night, dawn and dusk. Forages for crabs and occurs whenever they are plentiful; when alarmed, it flies with a croaked *querk*, often repeated and higher pitched than the Black-crowned Night-Heron. Nests in pairs and small colonies; large rough nests in trees at low elevation, clutch 2–4, February to May. Adults and immatures seen in equal numbers in fall and winter.

Status. Fairly common breeding resident in the three Islands; migrants from North America also occur in winter.

FAMILY THRESKIORNITHIDAE: IBISES and SPOONBILLS.
Two species of Ibis occur as rare passage migrants; the Spoonbill is a vagrant (Appendix 2). Fly like storks with neck extended. Sexes alike.

WHITE IBIS   *Eudocimus albus*

Field characters. 64cm:25in Large. Adult: *entirely white except for black tips to wings* (four primaries); long *reddish decurved bill; facial skin and legs scarlet.* Immature: dark brown upperparts; paler streaking on head and neck; white underparts and rump; *pinkish bill and legs.* Legs project beyond tail in flight.

Range. Greater Antilles, southern United States to northern South America.

Cayman habitat. Lagoons and secondary swamps.

Status. Rare in passage, Grand Cayman; very rare, Cayman Brac and Little Cayman; birds (usually singletons) occasionally over-winter, July to May. The AOU lists the species as mainly sedentary, so the Cayman records are probably the result of post-breeding dispersals from nearby islands in the Greater Antilles.

GLOSSY IBIS *Plegadis falcinellus*

Field characters. 60cm:23in Appears black in flight and in the field; *long decurved dark olive bill and blackish olive legs in all plumages.* Breeding: chestnut brown body; metallic greenish purple gloss on wings and back. Non-breeding: duller; brown streaking on neck. Immature: brownish; white streaking on head and neck.

Range. Greater Antilles, North America to northern South America. Cosmopolitan.

Cayman habitat. Lagoons; flooded grassland; the Ironshore.

Habits. Distinctive silhouette in flight with curved bill and neck outstretched.

Status. Rare passage migrant and short-stay winter visitor in the three Islands; records in all months.

FAMILY ANATIDAE: DUCKS. Flattened bills and webbed toes; many have a brightly coloured speculum on the inner wing. Only one species breeds, and four species are regular migrants; see also Appendix 2.

FULVOUS WHISTLING-DUCK *Dendrocygna bicolor*

Field characters. 49cm:19in Similar outline and flight pattern to the West Indian Whistling-Duck. Adult: back dark brown, feathers tipped with tawny; neck streaked; face, breast and underparts *unmarked cinnamon; buffy white streak along sides; white rump. In flight shows blackish unmarked upper and under wings; white upper tail.*

Range. West Indies, North, Central and South America. Africa and Asia.

Cayman habitat. Lagoons and ponds.

Habits. Call: 2 syllable *wu-cheu.*

Status. Presently very rare passage migrant (mainly in fall) and casual short-stay winter visitor in the three Islands. This species is still expanding its range in the region and more sightings can be expected.

WEST INDIAN WHISTLING-DUCK (Whistler)
Dendrocygna arborea   **Plate 28**

Field characters. 53cm:21in A long legged, long necked upright duck, similar to a goose. Chestnut brown forecrown, rising to a blackish hindcrown; blackish stripe down nape to back; upper face pale ginger; lower face and sides of neck grey; chin and throat whitish; lower neck and breast a rich tawny chestnut with black streaks; rich brown on back and wings with pale edges to feathers; rump and tail blackish; *dramatic black and buff markings on sides and flanks;* underparts whitish heavily spotted with black; bill, legs and feet black. *In flight legs project behind tail;* head and neck are held low; dark unmarked under wings and a *silvery buff patch on the primary coverts of the upper wing.* Sexes alike.

Range. Cayman Islands, Greater Antilles and the Bahamas.

Cayman habitat. Grand Cayman: roosts and breeds in the Central Mangrove Swamp and in Buttonwood swamps; forages on lagoons, secondary swamp and freshwater ponds. Breeds throughout the swamps and on the bluffs, Little Cayman and Cayman Brac. Nests are often built on Ironshore outcrops in lagoons.

Habits. In Grand Cayman, the ducks fly out after dusk

from their day roost to their nocturnal feeding grounds, returning to the mangrove before dawn; flight call a haunting 4–5 syllable whistle *shir-ee* (rising)-*eee-srr-srrr* (falling). In Little Cayman, where the population has increased, ducks feed throughout the day especially on Booby Pond and Charles Bight Ponds. Clutch 5–13, in large rough nests on or near the ground; breeding throughout the year.

Status. The only duck to breed in the Islands, a protected species listed as endangered. Uncommon breeding resident, Grand Cayman; although in the mid 1990s over 100 birds were regular at Willie Ebanks' farm at Hutland, North Side, believed to represent a large part of the total population. Common, Little Cayman. Small breeding population re-established in 1993, Cayman Brac.

MALLARD   *Anas platyrhynchos*

Field characters. 61cm:24in Male: *green head and neck with white collar; chestnut breast;* grey back, sides and abdomen; black tail with white terminal band; yellow bill. Female: mottled brown and buff. Both show dark blue speculum, with white trailing edge in flight. Eclipse male resembles female.

Range. North America; winters to Mexico and western Cuba.

Cayman habitat. Lagoons.

Status. Casual, Little Cayman. A flock introduced in Grand Cayman in 1982, which became feral, has not been observed in recent years.

BLUE-WINGED TEAL   *Anas discors*

Field characters. 39cm:15in Small duck. Male breeding: *white crescent in front of eye;* dark crown and nape; grey face and neck; white flank patch; speckled brown plumage. Male returns from North America in eclipse plumage (same colour as female) and only acquires breeding plumage in December. Female: speckled brown and buff. Both sexes show a *green speculum and light blue wing coverts in flight;* dark bill; yellowish legs and feet. Immature: brown plumage similar to female until mid-January. (Note: the vagrant Green-winged Teal shows no blue on wing coverts in flight.)

Range. North America; winters to the West Indies, Central and South America.

Cayman habitat. All wetland lagoons and ponds; fresh-water ponds, Grand Cayman.

Habits. Most frequently seen duck; pairs on most permanent and temporary ponds, unperturbed by noise and people; dabbles with head under water for weed and insects; flies straight up out of the water when disturbed hence the name 'springing duck'.

Status. Common winter visitor and passage migrant, Grand Cayman and Little Cayman; common to fairly common, Cayman Brac; mainly August to April but records in all months. Overall numbers have decreased since the 1980s.

NORTHERN SHOVELER *Anas clypeata*

Field characters. 47cm:19in Very wide, *long, flattened bill* appears joined to head at the crown; orange legs. Male breeding: iridescent blackish green head and neck; *white breast and flank patch;* chestnut sides and abdomen; black back and rump; black bill. Female: speckled brown and buff. In flight resembles the Blue-winged Teal; both adults have light blue wing coverts (show white at a distance) and a green speculum, the male has *dark unmarked head and white breast.*

Range. North America; winters to the West Indies, Central America and northern South America. Europe and Asia.

Cayman habitat. Wetland lagoons and ponds; flooded marl pits, Grand Cayman.

Habits. Like the Blue-winged Teal springs out of the water, the wings making the same sound. Swims with neck hunched and bill at 30° angle to water. Male in full plumage by September.

Status. It has become uncommon in passage (chiefly in fall) and rare in winter in the three Islands, mainly September to April.

AMERICAN WIGEON   *Anas americana*

Field characters. 50cm:20in Male breeding: *rounded head with whitish crown;* small blue bill with black tip; *iridescent green patch from eye to nape;* grey brown upperparts; speckled grey face and neck; brownish chestnut breast and sides; *white abdomen and flank patch.* Eclipse male and breeding female: *grey speckled head* and brownish plumage. In flight, both show *green speculum* and male shows broad *white upper wing-coverts and pale head.*

Range. North America; winters to the West Indies, Central America and northern South America.

Cayman habitat. Wetland lagoons and ponds throughout, regular on Meagre Bay Pond and Colliers Pond, Grand Cayman.

Status. Increasingly uncommon winter visitor (only a few pairs over-winter) and passage migrant in the three Islands, August to May with the majority from November to March.

LESSER SCAUP   *Aythya affinis*

Field characters. 42cm:16.5in Male breeding: appears *black, white, black in the field;* black head and neck with purplish sheen; black breast; back and sides whitish grey (finely barred black and white); black rump and tail; beady yellow eye; pale bill. Female: dark brown with a *white ring at base of blue bill.* Both male and female: peaked hindcrown; in flight show *white stripe on inner secondaries* and a white abdomen contrasting with dark head and breast. Immature: duller than adults, brown eye.

Range. North America; winters to the West Indies, Central America and northern South America.

Cayman habitat. Lagoons and ponds throughout, regular, Meagre Bay and Pease Bay Ponds, Grand Cayman and westerly ponds, Cayman Brac; freshwater, cat-tail and sedge ponds, Grand Cayman.

Status. Uncommon winter visitor in the three Islands, October to April, the majority arrive in November; and a few birds occur in passage.

FAMILY CATHARTIDAE: AMERICAN VULTURES.
Only one species has been recorded.

TURKEY VULTURE (John Crow)   *Cathartes aura*

Field characters. 75cm:30in Adult: large, blackish brown; black wings held in a *shallow V during soaring flight* show silvery primaries and secondaries; bald red head and red feet; long tail. Immature: dark head. Sexes alike.

Range. Greater Antilles, the Bahamas and throughout the Americas.

Cayman habitat. Woodland, eastern bluff, Cayman Brac. Coastal and urban, Grand Cayman.

Status. Non-breeding. One or two birds as rare intermittent residents, Grand Cayman; 1 to 4 birds resident since 1982 with occasional absences, Cayman Brac; no records for Little Cayman.

FAMILY ACCIPITRIDAE: HAWKS AND EAGLES.
Raptors with strong talons and hooked bills. Two species are regular winter migrants; there are no breeding raptors in the Islands, apart from the Barn Owl.

OSPREY (Fish Hawk)   *Pandion haliaetus*

Field characters. 58cm:23in Very large raptor. Adult: *bright white head* with blackish streaks on crown, slightly crested; *blackish patch from eye to nape;* females may show dark collar below throat; dark blackish brown back and wings. Overhead, flies with wings bent showing *two black carpel patches, white underparts and under wing-coverts.* Sexes alike. Immature: pale edges to mantle and wing feathers.

Range. Cuba, Bahamas, Virgin Islands, North and Central America; North American birds winter to the West Indies and South America. Cosmopolitan.

Cayman habitat. Forages along marine sounds and fringing reefs, on lagoons and perches on favoured emergent trees in coastal woodland and mangrove year after year. Also forages at the airport and on the bluff, Cayman Brac.

Habits. Usually seen singly or in pairs, with small groups in migration. Spectacular feeding dives, hitting the water feet first, plunging partially under the surface to emerge shaking feathers with fish held lengthwise in its talons; also occasionally takes egrets at the airport, Cayman Brac. Call: a far carrying *s-ee-u,* repeated.

Status. Uncommon to fairly common winter visitor and passage migrant in the three Islands, September to May, but records in all months. One bird was resident on Little Cayman since before 1982 to 1988, when a hurricane damaged its roosting habitat.

NORTHERN HARRIER   *Circus cyaneus*

Field characters. 53cm:21in Both adults: *owl-like face; white rump;* long narrow tail; small bill. Adult male: *dark grey upperparts;* whitish underparts; black tips to primaries. Female: *dark brown upperparts;* tawny underparts streaked on breast and flanks; brown banded tail. The immature male is similar to the female but has brighter cinnamon underparts streaked with dusky brown.

Range. North America; winters to the West Indies and northern South America. Europe and Asia.

Cayman habitat. Open land; lagoons and secondary swamp; low coastal mangrove.

Habits. Flies with wings in a shallow V, tilting and turning as it comes low to hunt, silent.

Status. Rare short-stay winter visitor and passage migrant in the three Islands, July to April, with the majority from November to March.

FAMILY FALCONIDAE: FALCONS. Three migrant species have been recorded.

AMERICAN KESTREL (Killyhawk)   *Falco sparverius*

Field characters. 28cm:11in Both sexes: slate grey head; rufous crown patch; white face with *two black vertical bars* behind and below eye; white throat; cinnamon breast; whitish abdomen; rufous back barred with black (less bars on male); small, hooked black-tipped bill. Male: *grey wings* spotted with black; blackish spots/streaks on sides; *unbarred* rufous tail with black sub-terminal band and white tip. Female: *rufous wings* barred with black; cinnamon brown streaks on breast; *brown barred tail;* conspicuously larger than male. Sexes also differ in juvenile plumages. Softer outline, longer tail and narrower wings than the Merlin.

Range. West Indies, North and South America; North American birds winter in the West Indies.

Cayman habitat. Cleared land and urban areas; the edge of inland and coastal woodland; secondary mangrove.

Habits. Perches on wires and dead trees to watch for insects (main food source), catches dragonflies on the wing; hovers and dives to take lizards on the ground; pursues small birds in the air, often mobbed by other birds. Call: high *killy-killy-killy.* Bobs head.

Status. Fairly common winter visitor, Grand Cayman and Cayman Brac; uncommon, Little Cayman; mainly October to April. Cyclical fluctuation in numbers.

MERLIN   *Falco columbarius*

Field characters. 30cm:12in Stocky, angular falcon with broad wings, sharply pointed in flight; yellow feet and legs. Male: plain *dark bluish grey upperparts;* lower face, chin and throat whitish, *one vertical black line below eye; pale underparts heavily streaked brown;* 4 grey bands on blackish tail. Female and immature: *dark brown upperparts* with same streaked underparts as male; tail brown with light bands. Great variation in colour on back and breast from light to very dark.

Range. North America; winters to the West Indies and northern South America. Europe and Asia.

Cayman habitat. Lagoons and secondary swamp; open fields; shores; woodland.

Habits. Aggressive and usually solitary. Very fast direct flight with powerful downward wing stroke, skims over top of vegetation; angles wings more than Kestrel. Hunts from a perch and take insects; also courses, suddenly appearing low over waders feeding on lagoons; pursues swallows and small birds over open fields. Silent. Appears dark in the field; size and flight similar to a dove.

Status. Fairly common winter visitor and passage migrant in the three Islands, July to May, with the majority from October to March. Numbers fluctuate from year to year.

PEREGRINE FALCON   *Falco peregrinus*

Field characters. 50cm:20in Thickset, heavy in front with long tapering wings; powerful smooth flight with short wing-beats, interspersed with glides; great acceleration and manoeuvrability. Adult: *black head and nape joining pronounced vertical* *bar below eye, forming a helmet;* blackish back; barred tail; underparts buff to tawny, heavily streaked with black; long sweptback pointed wings; bright yellow legs. Plumage varies from light to very dark depending on breeding range. Immature: brown upperparts and barred tail.

Range. North America; winters to the West Indies and as far south as Chile, South America. Cosmopolitan.

Cayman habitat. Open disturbed habitat; lagoons and secondary swamp; woodland and bushland.

Habits. Perches on tall tree to select prey; courses with a very fast flight, striking ducks, gulls, waders and egrets as they take to the air, also occasionally attacking on the ground; dives to strike birds flying below.

Status. Uncommon winter visitor and passage migrant in the three Islands, September to May, with some arrivals in December and January.

FAMILY RALLIDAE: RAILS. Water birds with laterally compressed bodies; long legs and feet; run over surface of water. Four species occur, two are breeding residents.

SORA   *Porzana carolina*

Field characters. 23cm:9in A small rail. Adult: *short thick yellow bill;* large olive yellow legs and feet; no frontal shield; brownish upperparts, finely streaked black and white; grey sides to face, neck and breast; whitish abdomen; brown and buff barring on sides and flanks; short pointed tail shows yellowish under tail-coverts. Male breeding: *front of eye, lores and elongate patch from chin to upper breast, black.* Immature lacks black markings, also reduced in females and non-breeding males.

Range. North America; winters to the West Indies, Central and South America.

Cayman habitat. Near cover on secondary swamps and lagoons; freshwater pond edges, Grand Cayman.

Habits. Secretive; constantly flicks tail; alarm call: *wheet.*

Status. Uncommon (and hard to see) winter visitor, Grand Cayman and Little Cayman; very rare in passage, Cayman Brac; September to May, with the majority from October to March.

PURPLE GALLINULE   *Porphyrula martinica*
   Plate 29

Field characters. 33cm:13in Adult: *brilliant violet blue head and underparts;* bronze green back and wings; *frontal shield powder blue;* bill red with yellow tip; legs and feet yellow; *under tail-coverts entirely white.* One of the most beautiful birds in the Islands. Immature: entirely brownish olive including bill; shield dull brown; distinguished from immature Common Moorhen by absence of white side stripe.

Range. Cayman Islands, West Indies, the Bahamas, North, Central and South America.

Cayman habitat. Breeds and roosts in dense cover in mangrove and Buttonwood swamps; freshwater ponds including Governor's Pond, Grand Cayman. Migrants occur throughout wetlands and along coastal littoral.

Habits. Resident birds are normally shy, rapidly making for cover; in contrast arriving migrants appear unafraid, walking openly on roads and coastal areas. Calls: cackles and squawks like a Moorhen but shriller and does not descend. Nests near water, clutch 3–12, May to October.

Status. Uncommon breeding resident, Grand Cayman; probably resident, Little Cayman but no breeding records for Little Cayman or Cayman Brac. Cyclical variation from uncommon to locally common in migration in the three Islands, April to July.

WHITE-TAILED TROPICBIRD 54

WHITE-TAILED TROPICBIRDS (54)

BROWN BOOBY 55

RED-FOOTED BOOBY:
BROWN MORPH 55

14

RED-FOOTED BOOBY: 55
WHITE MORPH

MAGNIFICENT FRIGATEBIRD:
BREEDING MALE 58

MAGNIFICENT FRIGATEBIRD:
MALE, FEMALE, NESTING (58)

16

MAGNIFICENT FRIGATEBIRD:
IMMATURE (58)

SNOWY EGRET:
BREEDING PLUMAGE 63

LITTLE BLUE HERON:
ADULT 64

19

LITTLE BLUE HERON:
IMMATURE **64**

TRICOLORED HERON:
ADULT 65

21

TRICOLORED HERON: IMMATURE 65

CATTLE EGRET:
ADULT 66

24

CATTLE EGRET:
BREEDING PLUMAGE 66

GREEN HERON 67

YELLOW-CROWNED NIGHT-HERON:
ADULT (68)

26

YELLOW-CROWNED NIGHT HERON:
IMMATURE 68

**WEST INDIAN WHISTLING-DUCK:
ADULT** **71**

PURPLE GALLINULE:
ADULT 80

COMMON MOORHEN:
ADULT 145

COMMON MOORHEN:
IMMATURE (145)

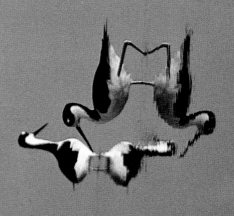

BLACK-NECKED STILT:
ADULT (149)

WILLET:
BREEDING PLUMAGE 152

LEAST TERN:
BREEDING PLUMAGE (166)

WHITE-CROWNED PIGEON:
BREEDING PLUMAGE (170)

WHITE-WINGED DOVE:
ADULT 171

38

ZENAIDA DOVE:
ADULT 171

COMMON GROUND-DOVE:
ADULT 172

41

CARIBBEAN DOVE:
ADULT 173

CUBAN PARROT:
GRAND CAYMAN SUB-SPECIES

175

CUBAN PARROT:
CAYMAN BRAC AND LITTLE CAYMAN SUB-SPECIES

MANGROVE CUCKOO:
ADULT **177**

INSET:
MANGROVE CUCKOO

45

44

SMOOTH-BILLED ANI (177)

BARN OWL

48

ANTILLEAN NIGHTHAWK:
MALE 180

WEST INDIAN
WOODPECKER: (182)
MALE

49

NORTHERN FLICKER:
MALE 183

NORTHERN FLICKER:
FEMALE **183**

CARIBBEAN ELAENIA:
ADULT 184

INSET: IMMATURE

53

52

INSET:
WINTER ADULT

56

LA SAGRA'S FLYCATCHER 185

LOGGERHEAD KINGBIRD:
BREEDING ADULT 187

RED-LEGGED THRUSH:
ADULT 194

61

NORTHERN MOCKINGBIRD:
ADULT (195)

THICK-BILLED VIREO:
ADULT (197)

BLACK-WHISKERED VIREO:
ADULT 199

YUCATAN VIREO:
ADULT 199

64

YUCATAN VIREO:
ADULT 199

VITELLINE WARBLER:
GRAND CAYMAN SUB-SPECIES 208

INSET:
VITELLINE WARBLER:
GRAND CAYMAN SUB-SPECIES

68

VITELLINE WARBLER:
CAYMAN BRAC AND LITTLE CAYMAN SUB-SPECIES 208

BANANAQUIT:
ADULT 217

INSET:
IMMATURE

71

STRIPE-HEADED TANAGER:
MALE 218

CUBAN BULLFINCH.
MALE 221

CUBAN BULLFINCH:
FEMALE **221**

YELLOW-FACED GRASSQUIT:
MALE 222

77

GREATER ANTILLEAN GRACKLE:
MALE (224)

COMMON MOORHEN (Red Seal Coot) *Gallinula chloropus* **Plates 30, 31**

Field characters. 33cm:13.5in Adult breeding: head and neck charcoal black; back brownish black; bright *red bill tipped with yellow, pronounced red frontal shield;* slaty underparts; *white band along sides in all plumages;* two white under tail-covert flashes on black tail; long greenish legs with red tibial bands. Adult non-breeding: plumage becomes browner in early winter. Out of water, moorhens are shaped like young domestic chickens. Black fluffy chicks with red facial skin. Immature: greyish brown; dull frontal shield and brown bill; olive legs.

Range. Cayman Islands and West Indies. Cosmopolitan.

Cayman habitat. All habitats near water, including garden ponds.

Habits. Moves head back and forward and flicks tail when swimming; runs across top of water for cover. Calls: very noisy when alarmed, making a series of loud harsh crackles *ke ke ke ke ka ka kaa kaaa* descending and suddenly silent; also a single questioning *cluck* repeated. Clutch 1–12, low nest near water; breeding in all months.

Status. Breeding resident in the three Islands; very common, Grand Cayman; common, Cayman Brac and Little Cayman where numbers are increased by migrants in winter.

AMERICAN COOT *Fulica americana*

Field characters. 39cm:15in Large rail. Adult: black head and neck; charcoal grey body; *large white bill with dull red sub-terminal band;* the small dull red frontal shield is raised but hard to see; red eye; outer under tail-coverts white; greenish legs and feet with lobed toes. Shows white trailing edge to wing in flight. Immature: paler than adult; whitish underparts.

145

Range. Greater Antilles, the Bahamas and North to South America. North American birds winter in the breeding range, West Indies, and Central America to northern South America.

Cayman habitat. Mangrove lagoons and ponds; freshwater and sedge ponds, Grand Cayman.

Habits. In pairs or small groups, often with moorhen or teal. Call: *kuk kuk kuk.*

Status. Fairly common to locally common winter visitor in the three Islands. There is one January breeding record in Cayman Brac where the parent was an intermediate (see below); both parent and young migrated in May.
Note. The Caribbean Coot, *F. caribaea*, previously thought to be a separate species, is often regarded as a colour morph of the American Coot; inter-breeding has been recorded in the Antilles resulting in intermediates in colouration. (Bond pers. comm.).

FAMILY CHARADRIIDAE: PLOVERS. Chunky
waders with short bills and large eyes; sexes alike; many run in short bursts along shores and mud flats; surface feeders. Four species occur as regular migrants.

BLACK-BELLIED PLOVER *Pluvialis squatarola*

Field characters. 30cm:12in Our largest plover. Breeding plumage (April to August): pale grey crown; black and pale grey upperparts; white forehead and superciliary stripe continues to white nape and shoulders; black face, breast and abdomen; *white under tail-coverts;* short heavy black bill; dark legs. Non-breeding adult and immature: pale grey mottled upperparts; whitish underparts; large black eye and dark patch on ear coverts. In early fall and late spring moulting birds show face and underparts mottled with black. In all seasons *in flight shows black axilla (armpits); broad white band across primaries and secondaries; white rump and upper tail; tail barred distally.*

Range. Arctic; winters to the West Indies, North to South America. Cosmopolitan.

Cayman habitat. Reefs and shores; secondary swamp, lagoons and pond edges.

Habits. Stationary birds; sit for long periods with neck on shoulders; appear whitish grey in the field in winter. Calls: *tlee*, and a plaintive far-reaching *klee-u-ee* in flight.

Status. Very common passage migrant and the most common wader in winter in the three Islands, mainly July to May with a few recorded in June.

LESSER GOLDEN-PLOVER   *Pluvialis dominica*

Field characters. 27cm:10.5in Breeding: black upperparts flecked with gold and white; white superciliary stripe continues to nape and sides of breast; black face and underparts. Non-breeding: dark brownish grey upperparts may be mottled with gold; pale brownish grey breast, whitish abdomen. Smaller than Black-bellied Plover with a darker crown; bill shorter and thinner; in *flight shows pale axilla; dark rump, tail and wings.*

Range. Arctic; winters in South America. Cosmopolitan.

Cayman habitat. Secondary swamp; flooded grassland; rocky shores.

Status. Rare passage migrant in fall and spring, occasionally a short-stay winter visitor, August to May.

WILSON'S PLOVER   *Charadrius wilsonia*

Field characters. 20cm:8in Breeding male: greyish brown upperparts; wide black breast band; black lores and frontal bar. Breeding female and non-breeding male: black replaced by lighter brown upperparts and breast-band. All adults: larger than Semipalmated Plover with a *large head and long,* *heavy black bill;* shorter wing-bar in flight; *greyish pink legs;* white forehead continues as superciliary to eye; white collar around hindneck; white underparts. *Wide breast-band* and colour and shape of bill are best field marks.

Range. West Indies, North, Central and South America.

Cayman habitat. Shores including rocky headlands; dry lagoon edges; sandy tracks.

Habits. Slower moving than Semipalmated Plover and often solitary. Calls: slight high pitched *weeet,* also a lower double *qu-it.*

Status. Uncommon in passage in the three Islands in all months. Breeds throughout the Greater Antilles; reported as breeding here in the early part of the century.

SEMIPALMATED PLOVER   *Charadrius semipalmatus*

Field characters. 18cm:7in Breeding male, April to September: brown hindcrown and back; black frontal bar separates white forehead from crown and joins black line from bill to ear coverts; short whitish superciliary behind eye; white collar around hindneck; white underparts with single narrow black breast-band (ear coverts and breast-band brownish in females); *short, rounded yellow bill tipped with black,* yellow orange legs. Immature and non-breeding adult: *similar but bill blackish or black; black face markings and breast-band (often incomplete) become olive brown,* superciliary continuous with white forehead. In flight shows long white wing-bar and entirely white under wings.

Range. Arctic; winters to the West Indies, North, Central and South America.

Cayman habitat. Lagoon and pond edges; sandy roads; shores including headlands; disturbed habitats.

Habits. Call: *koo-lee* short, rising on second syllable.

Status. Common passage migrant and locally common

winter visitor in the three Islands, July to May; peak months are August to October, December to January, May. A few birds occur in June.

KILLDEER   *Charadrius vociferus*

Field characters. 25cm:10in Large, long-bodied plover. Breeding: brownish crown and back; blackish face pattern; white forehead and superciliary stripe; orange eye-ring; *two black or blackish breast-bands;* white collar around hindneck; white underparts; black bill; pinkish or yellowish legs. Non-breeding adults and immatures: back rufous brown, breast-bands brown and black. In flight shows long wings and tail, long *white* wing stripe; *orange brown rump and upper tail-coverts* markedly visible on take-off and landing.

Range. West Indies, North and Central America and northern South America.

Cayman habitat. Shores; lagoons and secondary swamp; flooded grassland; brackish and freshwater swamps, Grand Cayman.

Habits. Calls: *kil-dee* or *kwil-ee* rising on second syllable; continuous alarm call *twee-tee-tee-tee.*

Status. Uncommon winter visitor and passage migrant in the three Islands, mainly September to May. A few birds occasionally over-winter.

FAMILY RECURVIROSTRIDAE: STILTS. Extremely long-legged waders.

BLACK-NECKED STILT (Tell Tale)   *Himantopus mexicanus*   **Plates 32, 33**

Field characters. 38cm:15in Adult: white except for black crown, hind neck, back and wings in male, back of female is brownish black. Both: long neck; long fine black bill; *extremely long, slender salmon pink legs*. Immature: brownish grey upperparts; greyish yellow legs. In flight appears black and white with red trailing legs and a greyish tail.

Range. Cayman Islands, West Indies, extreme eastern and south-western United States to South America.

Cayman habitat. Breeds and forages on lagoon and pond edges and inland wetlands, on Ironshore outcrops in secondary swamp; spoil banks; beside sedge ponds, Grand Cayman.

Habits. Wades up to abdomen and occasionally swims; occurs in pairs or groups with herons and other waders in feeding aggregates. Calls: noisy alarm, continuous *yip-yip-yip* on the ground and circling overhead, also *ki-eck,* often heard throughout the night. Adult shows distraction behaviour trailing a 'broken wing' to draw attention from young; clutch 1–4, on the ground in a shallow scrape, April to August.

Status. Common breeding resident, Grand Cayman and Little Cayman; small numbers breed in Cayman Brac where it is common in winter to early spring.

FAMILY SCOLOPACIDAE: SANDPIPERS. Slender waders, many with long bills for probing. Seventeen species are regularly recorded though only one species breeds.

GREATER YELLOWLEGS   *Tringa melanoleuca*

Field characters. 35cm:14in Breeding: upperparts speckled and spotted black, white and grey; face, long neck and underparts streaked; white abdomen. Non-breeding: upperparts grey; lower breast and abdomen white. All: *long robust bill slightly upturned; bright yellow legs;* pale eye-ring. In flight, dark wings, white rump with barred tail, and yellow legs show beyond tail.

Range. Northern North America; winters in the United States, West Indies, Central and South America.

Cayman habitat. Lagoons and ponds, secondary swamp; flooded grassland; freshwater swamps, Grand Cayman.

Habits. Wary; bobs head. Calls: *3–5* syllable *tcheu tcheu (tcheu) teu (teu)* descending, as it takes to the wing; also alarm *teu teu* . In feeding aggregates with stilts and herons; flocks up to 200 counted in migration.

Status. Common passage migrant and fairly common winter visitor in the three Islands, the majority from August to early April but records in all months.

LESSER YELLOWLEGS   *Tringa flavipes*

Field characters. 26cm:10.5in Similar to Greater Yellow-legs only *smaller*, with slimmer yellow legs and a *shorter finer straight bill.*

Range. As Greater Yellowlegs.

Cayman habitat. As Greater Yellowlegs.

Habits. Call: *teu*, 1–3 times, lower pitch than Greater Yellowlegs.

Status. Common to very common passage migrant and fairly common winter visitor in the three Islands, the majority from August to April but records in all months.

SOLITARY SANDPIPER   *Tringa solitaria*

Field characters. 22cm:8.5in Slender wader with *white eye-ring continuous with white loral stripe.* Breeding: dark olive brown upperparts speckled with white; streaked sides to neck, breast and sides; medium length blackish bill paler at base; white abdomen; *dark olive green legs.* Non-breeding: upperparts grey brown with less speckling. In flight shows dark wings and rump; *tail with dark central stripe and black and white bars* at outer edges.

Range. Northern North America; winters to the West Indies, Central and South America.

Cayman habitat. Prefers freshly flooded secondary swamp; grassy pools and rain pools on sandy roads; also moist open woodland; the Ironshore; lagoons and ponds.

Habits. Solitary; holds dark wings up over back then folds them slowly after alighting; dips heads; bounding flight. Call: 2 or 3 syllable *wheet weet (weet)*.

Status. Uncommon in passage, mainly in fall, and rare in winter in the three Islands, July to May.

WILLET (Laughing Jack)   *Catoptrophorus semipalmatus*
   Plate 34

Field characters. 39cm:15.5in Heavy body; long thick dark bill; white eye-ring; bluish grey legs. In flight, shows *black and white wing pattern above and below of black primaries crossed by wide white band to white secondaries; white rump; grey tail.* Breeding: entirely speckled and streaked grey, brown and black except for white superciliary, throat and abdomen. Non-breeding: pale greyish upperparts, whitish underparts.

Range. Cayman Islands, West Indies, North, Central and South America.

Cayman habitat. Lagoons and pond edges; shores. Nests behind the beach ridge and on lagoon edges and Ironshore outcrops in secondary swamps.

Habits. Occurs singly or in pairs; holds wings open above head displaying wing pattern and folds them slowly after landing; wades deep in water. Calls: flight call *pill-will-willet*, and an alarm *weik*. Nests, clutch 4, on the ground behind sandy beaches, May to July.

Status. Fairly common passage and winter migrant, and

152

fairly common to uncommon breeding species in summer in the three Islands; present throughout the year though there are thought to be separate migrant and breeding populations.

SPOTTED SANDPIPER   *Actitis macularia*

Field characters. 19cm:7.5in Small, chunky short-billed wader. Breeding, April to September; white underparts with large round *black spots;* pinkish bill with black tip. Non-breeding: spots absent, white underparts with *pale notch on shoulder;* olive brown upperparts; white superciliary stripe; black eye-line; white eye-ring; yellowish legs. In flight shows dark rump and tail barred at edges; *white stripe down mid-wing.*

Range. Northern North America; winters to the West Indies, Central and South America.

Cayman habitat. Mangrove lagoons, pond edges and secondary swamp; rain pools on sandy roads; the Ironshore.

Habits. Calls: 1 to 2 syllable *peet* or *weet weet,* repeated. Tips rump and tail up and down as it walks; in flight, glides and stiff wings beat from horizontal downwards.

Status. Fairly common winter visitor and passage migrant, locally common in late spring, in the three Islands, July to May with a few birds in June.

UPLAND SANDPIPER   *Bartramia longicauda*

Field characters. 30cm: 11.5in Small head and large body; *large dark eye in pale buffy face;* short yellowish bill; crown stripe; pale superciliary stripe; upperparts barred dark brown with pale edges to feathers; breast buffy with heavy streaks; rest of underparts white with chevrons along flanks; *long tail.* In flight, dark above, unmarked wings.

Range. North America; winters in South America. Cosmopolitan.

153

Cayman habitat. Rough grassland, around the airstrip, Cayman Brac, is a favoured site.

Habits. Shallow wing beat; wings held aloft on alighting showing white barred under wing-coverts.

Status. Very rare passage migrant in fall and spring, September and April records.

WHIMBREL *Numenius phaeopus*

Field characters. 43cm:17in Large wader with *long decurved bill (8–10cm:3–4in);* mottled brown upperparts; *dark crown with pale median stripe;* pale superciliary stripe; black eye-line; streaked neck and breast; whitish underparts; greyish legs and feet. Plumage unchanged throughout year. In flight appears grey overall.

Range. Northern North America; winters to southern United States, Central and South America, rarely in the West Indies. Europe and Asia.

Cayman habitat. Sandy shores; lagoon and pond edges.

Habits. Call: *T-t-t-t-t.*

Status. Rare passage migrant in the three Islands, mainly September to April but records in all months; a few birds occasionally over-winter and over-summer, Grand Cayman.

RUDDY TURNSTONE *Arenaria interpres*

Field characters. 21cm:8.5in Stocky short-legged wader with black pointed bill. Breeding male, March to September: *rusty orange and black back and wings; white with black pattern on head and neck; black breast-band;* white abdomen and rump; black patch on inner tail; short orange red legs. Breeding female: duller; blackish brown upperparts and breast-band. Non-breeding and immature: orange colour absent from upperparts; black and white replaced by dark brown on head and breast. Shows unmistakable *black and white striped pattern in flight* in all seasons.

Range. Arctic; winters to the West Indies and as far south as Chile. Cosmopolitan.

Cayman habitat. Ironshore and beaches; lagoons and small inland wetlands; disturbed habitats near water.

Habits. In pairs and small groups; surface feeder turning over stones. Calls: *cut-cut-cut* and slurred *trrrr-rip*.

Status. Common, very common in some years, migrant throughout the year, with the majority from July to May. Non-breeding birds resident at the Turtle Farm, Grand Cayman.

RED KNOT   *Calidris canutus*

Field characters. 27cm:10.5in Heavy, rounded wader. *Short medium length black bill;* short greenish legs. Breeding: upperparts patterned with black, brown and buff; *underparts and face cinnamon rufous.* Non-breeding: upperparts brownish grey with *white edges to feathers;* underparts whitish grey with streaks on neck and breast. In flight shows a narrow wing stripe and a pale grey tail.

Range. Arctic; winters to southern South America. Cosmopolitan.

Cayman habitat. Shores; lagoon edges with herbaceous cover.

Status. Rare in passage and casual in winter in the three Islands, July to May.

SANDERLING   *Calidris alba*

Field characters. 20cm:8in Breeding: rufous and black speckled upperparts and breast; white throat and abdomen; black legs; short bill. Non-breeding: very pale grey upperparts; white underparts; *black mark on shoulder.* In flight shows a *wide white* stripe on dark wings and white sides to tail.

Range. Arctic; winters to the West Indies, Central and South America. Cosmopolitan.

Cayman habitat. Sea edge on sandy shores; dry lagoon edges.

Habits. Compact flocks follow the to-and-fro wave motion at the sea edge; alarm call: *wit.*

Status. Infrequent, locally common short-stay migrant in the three Islands, July to May.

The following three very small sandpipers, called 'peeps', are very similar in non-breeding plumage; they frequent shores, beaches, rain pools and lagoon edges; show rapid flight in tight flocks. A specialist book (see Bibliog.) on waders is necessary to work out the graded series of plumages summarized here: breeding, new non-breeding, worn non-breeding, bright juvenile and faded/changing juvenile, and gradations in bill size.

SEMIPALMATED SANDPIPER   *Calidris pusilla*

Field characters. 16cm:6.25in Breeding: crown dark, streaked; *greyish upperparts with black centres and pale grey edges to mantle and scapular feathers* (may show rufous wash); tertials blackish brown with pale edges; *broad white superciliary in all plumages.* White underparts with brownish grey streaked neck and breast, sides and flanks; black legs; short straight black bill slightly expanded at the tip, longer in females (can be length overlap with the Western Sandpiper). Non-breeding: plain *greyish brown upperparts;* white underparts with *grey streaking at sides of breast.* Partially webbed toes. Juvenile: bright greyish buff; blackish mantle with pale edges to feathers and *rufous wash giving scaly effect;* diffuse streaking on sides of white breast. Narrow wing-bar in flight.

Range. Arctic; winters to the West Indies, Central and South America.

Cayman habitat. Sandy shores; lagoon, pond edges and secondary swamp.

Habits. Gregarious. Calls: short, loud *cherrk* and *kr-ei-p* on take-off.

Status. Passage migrant and short-stay winter visitor in the three Islands, July to May, abundant to fairly common in fall to mid-winter, major peaks in mid-September and October, uncommon in spring though minor peaks sometimes occur.

WESTERN SANDPIPER   *Calidris mauri*

Field characters. 17cm:6.5in Similar to Semipalmated, also with black legs and webbed toes; downcurved bill is longer. Breeding: upperparts grey, spotted black; rufous streaks on crown and ear coverts; *bright rufous on mantle and upper scapulars; greyish lower scapulars;* dark brown streaks and chevrons on white underparts. Non-breeding: greyer upperparts and whiter underparts than Semipalmated; *streaks on sides of breast may extend across.* Juvenile: rufous on upper scapulars contrasting with greyer lower scapulars; buffy wash on breast, sides streaked. White wing-bar in flight.

Range. Alaska; winters to the West Indies, Central and South America.

Cayman habitat. Prefers shores; lagoon and pond edges and coastal secondary swamp.

Habits. Single birds usual among flock of other peeps. Call: high thin *jeet.* May submerge head when feeding; probes deeply into mud.

Status. Rare but regular passage migrant in the three Islands, July to May, most often in fall and spring.

LEAST SANDPIPER   *Calidris minutilla*

Field characters. 14cm:5.5in Small size; *hunched outline; fine blackish bill slightly downcurved; yellowish legs* are the best field marks. Breeding: crown streaked brown and whitish with rufous; grey lateral crown and hindneck; dark lores and patch on ear-coverts; pale forehead; finely streaked superciliary;

157

streaked neck and breast-band on white underparts; mantle and scapulars have black-centred feathers with cinnamon edges and whitish tips (may form a V along edge of mantle); wing coverts greyish brown with buffy edges; *long tertials dark brown tipped whitish and buff.* Non-breeding: brownish grey upperparts and breast-band, *browner than other two peeps.* Juvenile: *bright chestnut on crown, feather edges of mantle, scapulars, wing coverts and tertials;* mantle edge whitish forming a V; *breast washed cinnamon with brown streaks;* wide white superciliary stripe to forehead. White wing stripe in flight.

Range. Alaska, Canada; winters to West Indies, Central and South America.

Cayman habitat. Prefers coastal and inland wetlands, freshly flooded secondary swamp; rain pools; rarely on shores.

Habits. Tame; calls: *tree-ee*, long or *treet* rising in a series.

Status. Very common passage migrant and fairly common winter visitor in the three Islands, July to May, with major peak in fall and minor peaks in December and spring.

WHITE-RUMPED SANDPIPER *Calidris fuscicollis*

Field characters. 19cm:7.5in. Larger than peeps. Bill blackish with yellowish base, short and slightly downcurved; long whitish superciliary; *long wings extend beyond tail at rest.* Breeding: upperparts variegated black, buff and grey washed with chestnut on head, nape and mantle; underparts white with greyish spots and streaking on neck and breast to flanks. Non-breeding: brownish grey upperparts; greyish streaks on breast, sides and flanks. Juvenile: similar to breeding adult only brighter, with contrasting dark crown and pale nape. In flight shows *broad white upper tail-coverts.* The majority are in pre-breeding plumage in spring migration.

Range. Arctic; winters in South America.

Cayman habitat. Lagoons.

Habits. Wades deep into water and submerges head. Call: *tzreet*, very high pitched, repeated.

Status. Locally common in late spring passage in May, and uncommon in fall in the three Islands, August to May.

PECTORAL SANDPIPER   *Calidris melanotos*

Field characters. 22cm:8.5in Similar to Least Sandpiper but larger. Adult: heavy body; *in all plumages heavy streaks on buffy breast end abruptly* (more dramatic in male) forming a sharp line with the white abdomen; short yellowish legs; *short slightly decurved bill* can appear bicoloured, yellowish at base and blackish brown distally. Breeding: upperparts dark brown edged with chestnut and buff; white throat. Non-breeding: brownish upperparts with dark centres to back feathers; pale edges to mantle. Juvenile: bright buff and chestnut on crown and edges to mantle; wide white superciliary stripe. In flight, dark above with a dark central stripe on white rump and tail; *white under wing-coverts contrast with dark breast and white abdomen.*

Range. Arctic; winters in South America.

Cayman habitat. Rocky headlands; lagoon edges and secondary swamp; rain pools.

Habits. Call: *trrip.*

Status. Uncommon to locally fairly common passage migrant in the three Islands, mainly in fall and early winter, with few spring records, July to May.

STILT SANDPIPER   *Calidris himantopus*

Field characters. 21cm:8.5in Appears large and long legged; *long white superciliary stripe;* long black *bill, thicker basally and slightly downcurved;* greenish legs. Breeding: dark brown back with rufous and whitish edges to feathers; *chestnut on crown, cheeks and ear coverts; complete underparts barred dark brown and white including sides and tail.* Non-breeding: brownish grey upperparts, *pale grey mantle with coverts edged white;* white underparts, streaked on breast and neck; *in flight shows white rump and upper tail.*

159

Range. Arctic; winters in South America.

Cayman habitat. Lagoons and secondary swamp.

Habits. Wades to top of legs, probing bill up and down or dabbles from side to side. Calls: *krrrt krrrt* and *wou*.

Status. Uncommon, locally common in some years, passage migrant, August to October and more rarely March and April; majority of records are from Grand Cayman.

SHORT-BILLED DOWITCHER *Limnodromus griseus*

Field characters. 30cm:12in Stocky bird with a very *long, straight, heavy blackish bill, paler at base;* white superciliary stripe; dark eye-line. Breeding plumage is beginning to fade when they arrive in fall: head streaked with cinnamon wash, back with black centres to feathers, pale and rufous edged; neck and breast cinnamon red with dark bars and spots; whitish abdomen; under tail-coverts barred. Non-breeding: grey brown crown and upperparts *with pale edges to feathers; whitish superciliary stripe;* greyish throat and breast; white abdomen; under tail-coverts spotted and barred; olive green to yellowish legs. In flight shows *white lower back in a wedge between wings; rump and tail barred and spotted.*

Range. Alaska and Canada; winters to the West Indies, Central and South America.

Cayman habitat. Lagoons, ponds, secondary swamps; brackish and freshwater swamps, Grand Cayman.

Habits. Small flocks feed and fly together; moves head up and down probing mud, most of bill remaining in water. Call: 3 short fluid notes *te-de-le*.

Status. Common passage migrant and fairly common winter visitor in the three Islands, July to May.

(**Note. LONG-BILLED DOWITCHER**, Appendix 2, can only be identified accurately in non-breeding plumage by its call: *keek*, singly or in a series.)

160

COMMON SNIPE   *Gallinago gallinago*

Field characters. 28cm:11in *Very long straight bill,* reddish at base, dark brown distally; *dark brown and buffy gold stripes on crown and face,* continue on dark back; speckled and barred neck, breast to flanks; white throat and abdomen; short olive legs. In flight shows *upper tail coverts barred; inner tail rufous, terminal band white.*

Range. North America; winters to the West Indies and North to South America. Europe and Asia.

Cayman habitat. Lagoons and secondary swamps; flooded grassland and sedge pond edges; regular around Governor's Pond and from Spotts to Bodden Town, Grand Cayman.

Habits. In low cover, either freezes or flushes just before being stepped on, exploding up in a zigzagging flight, with rattling wings and a harsh call: *caaap.*

Status. Uncommon to locally common passage migrant and winter visitor, Grand Cayman; rare in passage, Cayman Brac; October to April.

WILSON'S PHALAROPE   *Phalaropus tricolor*

Field characters. 23cm:9in All: small head; heavy bodied; long *very fine pointed bill;* white rump and upper tail-coverts in flight. Breeding female: dramatically marked; grey crown, nape and back; *black stripe from face down side of neck;* white throat and underparts; *chestnut on neck and breast;* black legs. Breeding male: paler with brown and grey upperparts. Non-breeding: *appears whitish in the field;* very pale grey upperparts; white face with black eye-line; white underparts; heavy yellow legs (July to December).

Range. North America; winters in southern South America.

Cayman habitat. Lagoon, pond edges and secondary swamps; freshwater ponds edges and rain pools, Grand Cayman.

Habits. *Very active agitated feeding behaviour is diagnostic:* dashes around or turns in circles either with head and neck submerged briefly raising them to swallow; also at pond and pool edges.

Status. Rare, most often single birds are regular passage migrants in fall and spring, Grand Cayman and Little Cayman; September to October, and March to May.

FAMILY LARIDAE: GULLS AND TERNS. Only the Least Tern breeds in summer; all other species are migrants or casual visitors. Despite the uncommonness of the majority of this family in the Cayman Islands all species are included in the text. This is to aid identification, which is often difficult as most species undergo at least four changes of plumage: first and second year immatures, breeding and non-breeding adults.

LAUGHING GULL *Larus atricilla*

Field characters. 40cm:16in Adult breeding: black head; white body and tail; *grey mantle and wings with black tips to primaries;* red bill and legs; broken white eye-ring; white trailing edge to wing in flight. Non-breeding and third winter: head white with brownish ear coverts and nape; *blackish* bill. Immature, first and second winter: back and wings brownish grey with blackish primaries; head darker than winter adult; breast greyish; abdomen white; *wide black terminal band on light tail.*

Range. West Indies, eastern North America to Central America and northern South America; winters to central South America.

Status. Locally common from winter to early summer, otherwise casual in all months and in all plumages, though breeding adults rare, around the coasts of the three Islands.

RING-BILLED GULL   *Larus delawarensis*

Field characters. 48cm:19in Pale gull. Adult breeding: heavy yellow bill with *black sub-terminal band;* plumage white; pale grey mantle and wings with *two white spots on black outer primaries* and white trailing edge; *legs yellowish;* white tail. Non-breeding adult: as breeding, except heavy spots on head and nape. Immature: first winter birds have black-tipped bill; *dark spotting on head, underparts and wings;* blackish primaries; *whitish inner tail with dark terminal band;* second winter birds have bill as adults; upperparts paler, heavy spotting on crown and nape; blackish primaries (no spots); *partial terminal tail band.*

Range. North America; winters in breeding range and to Mexico and the Bahamas, rarely to the Greater Antilles.

Status. Rare winter visitor in the three Islands, November to May; often in marine sounds.

HERRING GULL   *Larus argentatus*

Field Characters. 62cm:25in Very large. Adult breeding: white except for pale grey mantle and wings; *outer primaries black with white spots; bill yellow with red spot; legs flesh.* Non-breeding: brownish streaking on head and breast. Juvenile: entirely streaked grey brown; blackish bill; dark band to outer tail. Immature: becomes progressively lighter over three years with grey developing on wings; black tail band becoming reduced; blackish sub-terminal band on bill in second winter.

Range. North America; winters to the West Indies (southern edge of winter range), North and Central America. Cosmopolitan in northern Hemisphere.

Status. Uncommon to rare in winter and spring, mostly juveniles and immatures around coasts of the three Islands, October to May.

GULL-BILLED TERN   *Sterna nilotica*

Field characters. 35cm:14in Heavy body and broad wings. Breeding: black forehead to nape; silver grey back and wings appear white in flight with greyish edges to outer primaries; white face and underparts; *thick black bill;* black legs and feet; notched tail. Non-breeding: *white head with blackish around eye and ear coverts; nape may be streaked.* Juvenile: brownish speckled crown, nape and wings, darker primaries, all becoming lighter in first winter birds; blackish ear coverts.

Range. West Indies, North and Central America and coastal South America. Cosmopolitan.

Cayman habitat. Marine sounds and lagoons.

Habits. Call: *kee wak.*

Status. Rare in winter and in passage in the three Islands, records of single birds all months.

CASPIAN TERN   *Sterna caspia*

Field characters. 53cm:21in Largest tern. Breeding: *heavy red bill with dark tip;* black forehead, crown to nape; crested; grey wings show *dark outer primaries on underwing in all plumages* distinguishing it from Royal Tern. Non-breeding: *crown to nape streaked with white;* bill darker. Juvenile to second winter: brown scaling on scapulars; wings become paler; barring on outer tail reduces to grey.

Range. North America; winters in the breeding range and to northern South America, rarely to the West Indies. Cosmopolitan.

Status. Very rare in passage and in winter in the three Islands, September to April.

ROYAL TERN (Sprat bird)   *Sterna maxima*

Field characters. 51cm:20in The largest tern commonly seen around the Islands, usually in non-breeding plumage.

All: crested; pale grey back and wings with dark primaries; thick *entirely orange bill;* white underparts; forked tail; dark eye; black feet; appears white in the field except for *dark tips to outer primaries.* Breeding: black crested cap from forehead to nape, only held briefly in the breeding season. Non-breeding, July to May: *forehead and crown white with a black tonsure from behind the eyes;* bill yellow orange. First year immature: as non-breeding adult except bill, legs and feet yellowish; back and wings streaked brownish grey.

Range. West Indies, coastal United States, Central and South America. Africa.

Cayman habitat. Rocky headlands, fringing reefs, marine sounds.

Habits. Perches on mooring posts and sits on sandy beaches in small groups; plunge dives for fish. Call: *kee-er.*

Status. Resident, non-breeding; fairly common to common in the three Islands from August to May, a few birds in June and July.

SANDWICH TERN   *Sterna sandvicensis*

Field characters. 37cm:15in Adult: appears white in the field with a light graceful flight; *long black bill with yellowish tip in all adult plumages;* pale grey upperparts; dark edges to outermost primaries; white underparts; deeply forked tail. Breeding: black cap from forehead to nape, crested. Non-breeding: white forehead and forecrown; blackish from eye to hindcrown. Immature is similar except bill black; brownish on upperparts.

Range. Virgin Islands, Bahamas, Mexico and United States; winters throughout the West Indies, southeastern coast of North America and South America. Europe.

Status. Very rare in winter and in passage in the three Islands in coastal waters.

COMMON TERN   *Sterna hirundo*

Field characters. 38cm:15in Adult: grey upperparts; *whitish grey underparts; tail forked,* shorter than Forster's Tern; *darkly edged outer primaries.* Breeding: black cap from forehead to nape; bill red with black tip; red feet. Non-breeding: *black hindcrown and nape* forming a tonsure; white forehead; blackish bill. Immature: black patch on shoulder shows in flight as *blackish carpel bar* (leading edge to wing).

Range. Bahamas, Hispaniola to the Virgin Islands, North America; occurs throughout the year in the West Indies. Europe to Asia.

Status. Very rare in winter and in passage in the three Islands, around the coasts and lagoons.

FORSTER'S TERN   *Sterna forsteri*

Field characters. 35cm:14in Small tern. Adult: grey upperparts with *silvery white inner primaries in flight,* wings appear longer and paler grey than Common Tern; *white underparts;* long forked tail. Breeding: black cap from forehead to nape; *orange* bill with black tip; *orange* feet. Non-breeding: crown and nape whitish; *black band from eye to ear coverts only* distinguishes it from the Common Tern; blackish bill.

Range. North America; winters to the Greater Antilles, Bahamas and Central America.

Status. Rare in winter and in passage in the three Islands, mainly September to March, on lagoons.

LEAST TERN (Egg bird)   *Sterna antillarum*
Plate 35

Field characters. 23cm:9in A tiny white tern. Breeding: *white forehead to eye;* black crown, lores and nape; *yellow bill with black tip;* yellow legs; grey back and wings; blackish edges to outer primaries; white underparts; forked tail. Non-breeding:

bill becomes black; crown grey and streaked; black line through eye to nape; wings darker. Immature: brownish grey back; brown and white speckled head, black band from eye to nape; blackish bill; blackish shoulder bar on closed wing. Juvenile: upperparts buffy and white with brown curved markings on back; bill pale; shoulder bar.

Range. Cayman Islands, West Indies, North America.

Cayman habitat. Breeds on Ironshore outcrops in lagoons; areas near water altered by man (dry marl pits, spoil banks, sand bars). Regular on Meagre Bay Pond, Grand Cayman; Jackson's Pond, Little Cayman; Salt Water Pond and west end, Cayman Brac. Forages in shallow coastal waters, lagoons and freshwater ponds.

Habits. Flies like a swallow with fast wingbeats; hovers with head pointing downwards towards water before a plunge dive. Calls: *kre-ep*, also continuous *kit-kit-kit* when alarmed. Clutch 1–3, speckled eggs on bare ground, June to August.

Status. Fairly common, some years common, summer breeding visitor in the three Islands, April to October.

BRIDLED TERN   *Sterna anaethetus*

Field characters. 35cm:14in Adult: black crown and nape; black eye-line joins nape; *narrow white forehead extends past eye; white collar around hindneck;* white underparts; *white outer edges to forked tail; back and wings brownish grey;* bill and legs black. Immature: buff and grey back; greyish crown and sides; dark patch on ear coverts.

Range. West Indies and Central America. Cosmopolitan; pelagic species of tropical oceans.

Status. Very rare in passage in the three Islands, May to October, in marine sounds.

SOOTY TERN   *Sterna fuscata*

Field characters. 40cm:16in Similar to Bridled Tern but larger. Adult: black upperparts; *wide white forehead extends to eye only; collar absent;* white underparts; *forked tail black unlike Bridled Tern;* bill and feet black. Immature: sooty brown upperparts spotted with white; head and breast sooty brown; abdomen and underwings whitish.

Range. West Indies and Central America. Cosmopolitan; pelagic species of tropical oceans.

Status. Very rare in the three Islands, April to November, coastal.

BLACK TERN   *Chlidonias niger*

Field characters. 25cm:10in Breeding: *black head, neck and underparts;* dark grey back, wings and slightly forked tail; white under tail- and under wing-coverts. In fall and spring, arrives in the Islands with white and black mottling on head and underparts; during September the black is replaced by white. Non-breeding: white forehead; blackish crown, nape and ear coverts *separated by white collar from greyish patch in front of wing;* grey wings and tail; white underparts.

Range. North America; winters in South America. Europe and Asia.

Cayman habitat. Lagoons, ponds and secondary swamp; flooded marl pits.

Habits. Slow deep wing-beats on long pointed wings; dips prey from water's surface, hovers and may dive; perches on posts and roosts on the ground with waders. Usually silent.

Status. Fairly common to uncommon in passage in the three Islands, August to November, and April to June; winter records were the result of storms.

BROWN NODDY   *Anous stolidus*

Field characters. 40cm:16in Adult: entirely dark brown with a *white forehead and crown;* square notched tail; black bill and feet. Juvenile: dark forehead and crown; whitish tips to back and wing feathers.

Range. West Indies. Cosmopolitan; pelagic species of tropical oceans.

Status. Vagrant, see Appendix 2.

BLACK SKIMMER   *Rynchops niger*

Field characters. 48cm:19in Adult: blackish brown upperparts; long thick red bill, black distally, with *lower mandible longer;* white forehead and underparts. Immature: brown and white patterned upperparts; bill duller and smaller.

Range. North America to South America, casual in the Greater Antilles.

Cayman habitat. Marine sounds and sandy beaches.

Status. Very rare, casual in the three Islands in spring (March); one winter record following a storm.

FAMILY COLUMBIDAE: PIGEONS AND DOVES.
Six species occur including one endemic sub-species; two introduced species have established feral populations.

ROCK DOVE   *Columba livea*

Field characters. 33cm:13in Domestic pigeon, shows great colour variation from slate grey to brown and white.

Status. Introduced, Grand Cayman and Cayman Brac; small semi-feral populations breed in urban areas.

WHITE-CROWNED PIGEON (Bald pate)   *Columba leucocephala*   **Plate 36**

Field characters. 35cm:14in A large entirely charcoal grey pigeon except for *a white crown* and iridescent nape. Breeding male: crown (forehead to hindcrown) immaculate white. Breeding female: crown greyish white, reduced in extent. Immature: crown greyish.

Range. Cayman Islands, West Indies, South Florida and Keys.

Cayman habitat. Breeds and forages in mangrove; inland and coastal woodland and bushland. Sites of breeding colonies vary from year to year.

Habits. Very wary; mostly seen on the wing early and late when flocks fly between the inland feeding grounds and roosting sites. Breeding in colonies is usually synchronous, February to September, clutch 1–2, in large loose nests at 2–30 feet elevation. Call: in spring and summer, fast throaty *croo-cru (*rising*)-cura-croo* repeated, also *cru croo*. Favoured fruits include those of the Red Birch, Cinnamon Pepper, several species of Fig and Black Mangrove.

Status. Breeding in the three Islands. Numbers depend on the food supply: fairly common to abundant, February to September, with peaks from June to September when large numbers of migrants come through; uncommon, October to December. This highly mobile species flies between the three Islands and other islands in its range.

RINGED TURTLE-DOVE   *Streptopelia risoria*

Field characters. 30cm:12in Pale buffy grey; *black band around hindneck;* black primaries; *long tail;* plumage variable.

Status. Introduced, Grand Cayman and Cayman Brac; small feral populations breed close to urban areas.

WHITE-WINGED DOVE (White wing) *Zenaida asiatica*
Plate 37

Field characters. 30cm:12in Brownish cinnamon except grey abdomen and rump; crown and nape iridescent violet; *black malar whisker* under pale ear coverts; wide blue eye-ring; *white band along closed wing shows in flight as broad white band on the coverts;* tail with almost complete *white terminal band.*

Range. Cayman Islands, Greater Antilles, southern United States to western South America.

Cayman habitat. In all habitats except dense woodland; breeds mainly in mangrove; forages in disturbed and urban areas.

Habits. Forages in trees and on the ground; perches on telegraph wires; fast direct flight. Calls: *cru cruk ca roo,* a longer loud series of 8–10 phrases *cura-caa-cura-caa-cura,* and *cura croo.* Breed singly, in small groups and in loose colonies usually in mangrove, clutch 2, in loose nests, February to August.

Status. Increasingly common in migration and as a breeding resident, Grand Cayman (colonized about 1935 (Bond)) and Little Cayman (where it was confined to the west end up to 1985), the population increase is in response to increased disturbed habitat. Non-breeding, Cayman Brac, migrant feeding flocks now common in spring and summer, scarce in winter; as numbers increase it may eventually colonize.

ZENAIDA DOVE (Pea Dove) *Zenaida aurita*
Plate 38

Field characters. 28cm:11.5in Golden wash on cinnamon brown head; *dark blue mark above and below ear coverts;* sides of neck and rump iridescent violet; six to eight black spots on wing coverts; underparts vinaceous brown; white patch on wing *in flight shows as band on trailing edge of secondaries;* rounded tail with sub-terminal band black, *terminal band grey;* feet red.

Range. Cayman Islands, West Indies, coast of Central America; extirpated from Florida Keys.

Cayman habitat. Breeding in inland and coastal woodland and bushland and mixed woodland/Buttonwood swamps. In Grand Cayman occurs west of Savannah, regular at the Botanic Park and the Mountain Reserve.

Habits. Feeds almost entirely on the ground; pairs usual; often perches on low branches in woodland. Calls: throaty echoing *ku-ra (*rising) *ku coo coo* followed by a sighing *ooo ah (*rising) *ah.* Clutch 2, in shallow platform nests on the ground or low to mid-elevation in trees, March to October, peaks May to August.

Status. An increasingly uncommon breeding resident, eastern Grand Cayman, where it is under pressure from the successful colonizer, the White-winged Dove; common breeding resident, Cayman Brac and Little Cayman.

MOURNING DOVE   *Zenaida macroura*

Field characters. 30cm:12in Like Zenaida Dove but paler; *long pointed tail* with white sides; no white on wing in flight.

Range. Greater Antilles, North to Central America.

Cayman habitat. Disturbed habitat and pasture.

Status. Rare in passage in the three Islands, mainly in fall and spring, October to April.

COMMON GROUND-DOVE (Ground Dove)
Columbina passerina   **Plate 39**

Field characters. 17cm:6.5in The only small dove in the Islands, terrestrial. Pinkish cinnamon forehead, face and throat; pink bill with black tip; crown, nape and back speckled bluish grey; black spots on cinnamon brown wings; beautifully marked on breast and sides of neck with pinkish and grey feathers darkly edged, giving *a scaling effect*, most marked in breeding male; female paler. In brief flight before it resettles, short wings rattle and show *rufous primaries* and a black tail with white corners.

Range. Cayman Islands, West Indies, southern United States to South America.

Cayman habitat. Disturbed habitat including urban areas; dry open bushland; coastal habitat to the edge of the Ironshore; does not breed in mangrove or dense woodland.

Habits. Seen in pairs or small family groups; tame, only flies for a short distance when disturbed; searches for seeds with head bobbing; perches with tail drooped. Calls: varied *co-a* repeated, and *hoop*. Breeds throughout the year, peaking March-August, clutch of 2, in nest on the ground or low in shrubs and trees, often in Thatch or Coconut palms.

Status. Common breeding resident in the three Islands.

CARIBBEAN DOVE (White-belly) *Leptotila jamaicensis*
   Plates 40, 41

Field characters. 31cm:12.5in *Ivory forehead, throat, breast, abdomen* and under tail-coverts, becoming immaculate white when breeding; grey crown and nape; violet pink and bronze on hindneck to upper back; brownish pink sides of neck separated by white narrow line from wing; brown back, wings and tail; bill black; legs and feet red and fleshy. In flight shows three white tipped outer tail feathers and brown primaries on dark wings.

Range. Grand Cayman, Jamaica and coast and islands of Mexico; introduced on New Providence, Bahamas.

Cayman habitat. Breeds in inland woodland on Bluff Formation; forages in bushland and plantation edges, central and eastern Grand Cayman; readily seen at Hutland, the Mountain Reserve and the Botanic Park.

Habits. Terrestrial; walks over the pinnacled limestone which correlates with the well-developed legs; very approachable when eventually discovered and walks, rather than flies, away. Call: a long mournful *cru-cru-crooooo-coa* descending to a sobbing echo, repeated three times. Low nests, clutch of 2, March to July.

Status. Uncommon breeding resident, Grand Cayman; an endemic sub-species, *L. j. collaris* (Cory). Unconfirmed reports of this species calling on the bluff, Cayman Brac.

FAMILY PSITTACIDAE: PARROTS. There is one endemic Amazon species occurring as two endemic sub-species. Two introduced species, which have established feral breeding populations, have been included; as captive breeding success increases, more exotics may be expected to breed in the wild, see Appendix 2.

ROSE-RINGED PARAKEET   *Psittacula krameri*

Field characters. 40cm:16in Slim bird, green overall; *reddish bill;* shows *yellow under wing-coverts in flight.* Male: black chin; blue on nape; pink collar; *long tail with blue central feathers.* Female: shorter tail; male head colours replaced by green.

Habits. Call: sharp *keee-ek.*

Status. Introduced, Grand Cayman; small feral populations breeding around George Town and Savannah.

MONK PARAKEET   *Myiopsitta monachus*

Field characters. 28cm:11in Adult: green upperparts; whitish grey forehead and fore-crown, face, throat and iris (eye); *breast whitish grey, barred; yellowish abdomen;* long tail; *blue primaries; shows blue underwings in flight.*

Habits. Builds colonial roosting and breeding nests, often on telegraph poles; very noisy and gregarious.

Status. Introduced, Grand Cayman, feral populations breeding in George Town; resident, Savannah.

CUBAN PARROT (Parrot)   *Amazona leucocephala*
   Plates 42, 43

Field characters. 30cm:12in Both sub-species: *iridescent green feathers with dark edges* on crown, nape, back, wing coverts and underparts; wide whitish eye-ring; pale bill and feet; blue band on wing shows in flight as brilliant *blue primaries and secondaries;* under tail-coverts yellowish green; tail green with blue outer edges and red upper tail-coverts. Grand Cayman adult: *white forehead with rose blush; rose pink cheeks and throat; black ear coverts;* varied amounts of reddish pink on lower abdomen. The male is larger and more brightly coloured with the pink of the cheek patch and throat almost continuous. Juvenile: bright leaf green with dark edging to feathers absent; yellow forehead, crown, cheeks and throat become washed with pink; smaller than adult. Cayman Brac adult: smaller with more black on green feathers; white crown extends behind the eye and the rose blush is absent; under tail-coverts yellowish; extensive maroon area on abdomen; the juvenile is darker than the adult.

Range. Cayman Islands, Cuba, Bahamas.

Cayman habitat. Grand Cayman: breeding and roosting in mangrove and inland woodland; forages in all habitats including coastal woodland and urban areas, frequents North Sound Estates, Meagre Bay, the Botanic Park, the Mountain Reserve (protected breeding habitat) and Hutland. Cayman Brac: breeding in woodland on the bluff and foraging throughout the Island; seen regularly feeding on fruiting trees along Major Donald Drive, Stake Bay Road West, and in the two areas of protected breeding habitat. This sub-species occupies the smallest range of any amazon.

Habits. Detected by raucous squawking; feed in small flocks, though large flocks gather on fruit trees and before the breeding season; in flight appears black (unless in sunlight) with *blunt head and fast downward wingbeat,* fly in pairs; most active in the early morning and late afternoon, returning to roosting trees at dusk. Great variety of vocalizations: flight, perched and alarm calls. The Brac parrot is very secretive and more silent than the Grand Cayman sub-species; it has a different flight call: *d-dee, d-dee.* Nests in tree cavities, March to July, clutch 1–5, hatch in about 24 days and fledge at 6–8 weeks.

Status. A resident, with two endemic sub-species: *A. l. caymanensis* (Cory) is fairly common to common, Grand Cayman; *A. l. hesterna* (Bangs) is fairly common, Cayman Brac, though it appears invisible in early winter; it has been extirpated from Little Cayman. A protected endangered species for which breeding habitat has been purchased at the Mountain, Grand Cayman and on the bluff, Cayman Brac.

FAMILY CUCULIDAE: CUCKOOS AND ANIS. Two breeding resident species and one regular migrant occur, see also Appendix 2. Long tails and short rounded wings.

YELLOW-BILLED CUCKOO   *Coccyzus americanus*

Field Characters. 30cm:12in Similar to Mangrove cuckoo *except black eye mask absent,* yellow eye-ring; lower mandible almost entirely yellow; *underparts completely white;* shows bright *rufous inner primaries* in flight. Call similar.

Range. West Indies, North America to Central America; winters in South America.

Cayman habitat. Dry scrub; coastal woodland; mangrove.

Status. Uncommon, some years locally very common, passage migrant in the three Islands, August to November, and more often April to June; rare in winter, August to June.

MANGROVE CUCKOO (Rain bird) *Coccyzus minor*
Plates 44, 45

Field characters. 28cm:11.5in Long slender bird; hazel brown crown and upperparts; large eye covered with *black band to ear coverts;* bill long and downcurved, lower mandible usually shows blacker than Yellow-billed Cuckoo; white throat; breast to abdomen becoming an increasingly *rich yellow cinnamon;* perched, the long tail is black with white spots underneath, shows as black and white outer margins in flight. Immature: paler; incomplete face mask; buffy underparts; may resemble the Yellow-billed Cuckoo except *primaries are brown* not rufous.

Range. Cayman Islands, West Indies, Bahamas, south Florida, Central America.

Cayman habitat. Dry bushland; disturbed habitats; coastal and inland woodland; does not occur in mangrove in the Cayman Islands.

Habits. Scarce, heard more often than seen, often after rain; inactive and tame, often perched low under cover; short gliding flight. A surprisingly harsh extended call *ge-ge-ge-ge-gou-gou-gou-goul-goul* becoming slower and muffled. Nest usually under 10 feet, clutch 2–3, March-August.

Status. Uncommon breeding resident in the three Islands.

SMOOTH-BILLED ANI (Old/Black Arnold) *Crotophaga ani*   Plate 46

Field characters. 34cm:13.5in An unusual member of the cuckoo family. Adult: blue black plumage; iridescent bronze sheen on back and wings; *large horn-like bill with ridge on upper mandible curving above crown; very long tail,* equal to body length and widening distally; bare skin around eye; head and neck feathers are short, appearing scaly. Immature: smaller, dull black with brown edges to head, neck and back feathers. Often reported as a black parrot. The grackle is the only other large black bird, bill and tail distinguish them.

Range. Cayman Islands, West Indies, Florida, Central and South America.

Cayman habitat. Prefers disturbed habitat: grassland, roadsides and gardens, but occurs in all habitats.

Habits. Weak laboured flight; tail often thrown over back on landing; perches with wings drooped; noisy and gregarious, foraging in flocks of 5 to 8 or more, climbing clumsily over shrubbery and through grass in search of insects; frequently toppling over when wings get caught. Call: *keu-ik*, rising; also melodious warbling. Breeds throughout the year, rough nests, single pairs with clutch 2–8, and communal nest with clutch up to 17.

Status. A common breeding resident in the three Islands; very common, western Grand Cayman.

FAMILY TYTONIDAE: BARN OWLS. Heart shaped face and long legs; one species, a breeding resident, occurs.

BARN OWL (Screech owl)   *Tyto alba*
  Plate 47

Field characters. 40cm:16in The Cayman species is a very pale form, appearing white in the field; perched, the golden back and wing coverts are visible; dark eyes in a heart shaped face.

Range. Cayman Islands, West Indies. Cosmopolitan.

Cayman habitat. Open woodland; coastal habitat; urban areas and disturbed habitat.

Habits. Nocturnal. Perches along roadsides at dawn and dusk; silent flight on wide soft wings; feeds on rats, mice, bats, lizards and birds including woodpeckers, mockingbirds, bananaquits and grackles. Calls, hisses and clicks and a low chilling scream. Breeding throughout the year; clutch 2–8, nests in tree cavities, abandoned boats and cars, and caves in Cayman Brac and Little Cayman.

Status. Uncommon breeding resident in the three Islands.

FAMILY STRIGIDAE: TYPICAL OWLS. Only one species, a casual visitor, has been recorded.

SHORT-EARED OWL   *Asio flammeus*

Field characters. 38cm:15in Large, round dark face, orange eyes; upperparts and breast tawny and buff, streaked with black; pale abdomen; in flight shows two carpel patches, one black on the underwing, one pale on the upperwing.

Range. Greater Antilles, North America. Cosmopolitan.

Cayman habitat. Rough grassland close to water; airport and west end, Cayman Brac, is a favoured site.

Habits. Diurnal and terrestrial; perches in low bushes; irregular low gliding flight while hunting.

Status. Rare, casual, Cayman Brac and Grand Cayman. Also reported from Little Cayman over several years but no confirmed sightings.

FAMILY CAPRIMULGIDAE: NIGHTJARS. Crepuscular insectivores; one species occurs in the Cayman Islands as a summer breeding resident; two species occur in passage.

COMMON NIGHTHAWK   *Chordeiles minor*

Field characters. 22cm:9in Very similar to Antillean Nighthawk; overall colour more grey.

Range. North America to Central America; winters in South America.

Habits. Distinguished by call: *peent*.

Status. Rare passage migrant in spring and fall, Grand Cayman and Cayman Brac.

ANTILLEAN NIGHTHAWK (Rickery-Dick) *Chordeiles gundlachii* **Plate 48**

Field characters. 23cm:9in In flight a diagnostic *white band across outer primaries; long dark pointed wings;* notched tail. Adult perched: flat head with tiny bill; whitish superciliary stripe over large dark eye; upperparts beautiful autumn tones, speckled with buff, brown, russet, grey, black and white; grey V across scapulars; underparts buffy cinnamon barred with black. Male only: *white V on chin and upper throat; white band across tail.*

Range. Cayman Islands, Bahamas, Greater Antilles, southern Florida; winters to South America.

Cayman habitat. Breeds and forages in disturbed habitat including urban areas and dry marl pits; coastal littoral and the Ironshore.

Habits. Crepuscular; tumbles and swoops through the sky, hawking for insects; call diagnostic: *4–5 syllable rickery-dick* sound of the local name; perches lengthwise on tree branches or on the ground during the day. Breeding adults attempt to divert intruders by flying directly at them calling loudly; male dives steeply making a booming sound with its wings. Nest on stony or leaf-littered ground where the cryptic colouration makes the brooding adult very hard to see; clutch 1, June to August.

Status. Fairly common to locally common summer breeding visitor in the three Islands, March to late October.

CHUCK-WILL'S-WIDOW *Caprimulgus carolinensis*

Field characters. 30cm:12in *Large.* Brown and buff upperparts, streaked and spotted with black; *whitish throat band;* dark breast. Male only: white outer tail feathers in flight.

Range. North America; winters to the Greater Antilles, Bahamas and Central America.

Status. Very rare passage migrant in fall and in winter in the three Islands, in inland and coastal woodland.

FAMILY APODIDAE: SWIFTS. One species, an uncommon passage migrant, has been recorded.

CHIMNEY SWIFT   *Chaetura pelagica*

Field characters. 13cm:5in Small. Blackish grey upperparts; brownish underparts; buffy chin and throat; black band through eye; no tail; long wings curved backwards in an arc.

Range. North America; winters in South America.

Habits. Very rapid wing beats, flight *more like a bat than a bird*; feeds, bathes and drinks on the wing; twittering call.

Status. Uncommon to locally common passage migrant in the three Islands, often with swallows, August to November and February to June.

FAMILY TROCHILIDAE: HUMMINGBIRDS. There are no confirmed records of any members of this Family, though there are frequent unconfirmed sightings including one by the author. Bond suggested that the migrant Ruby-throated Hummingbird, *Archilochus colubris*, would be the most likely species to occur.

FAMILY ALCEDINIDAE: KINGFISHERS. Heavy billed, plunge divers; one species, a winter visitor, occurs in the Islands.

BELTED KINGFISHER (Kingfisherman)   *Ceryle alcyon*

Field characters. 32cm:12.5in Adult: slaty blue grey upperparts; large head with shaggy crest, frequently raised;

large, very heavy black bill; wide white collar around throat and neck; underparts *white except for broad grey breast-band;* erratic flight shows black wings with spotted white primaries. Female only: *rufous lower breast-band, sides and flanks.*

Range. North America; winters to the West Indies, Central and northern South America.

Cayman habitat. Coastal including the Ironshore edge; lagoons and ponds; freshwater ponds, Grand Cayman.

Habits. Perches motionless above water's edge, or hovers with bill pointed at water before a plunge dive for fish, also takes arthropods and crabs; very noisy with a wide range of long rattling calls.

Status. Fairly common winter visitor in the three Islands, late August to May.

FAMILY PICIDAE: WOODPECKERS. Birds adapted to forage on ants and termites and to drill out nest holes in trees; diagnostic undulating flight. There are two resident species confined to Grand Cayman; one migrant occurs throughout.

WEST INDIAN WOODPECKER (Red-head)
Melanerpes superciliaris   **Plate 49**

Field characters. 26cm:10.5in Male: *brilliant crown and nape;* pale forehead. Female: brilliant *red nape and hindneck;* grey forehead and crown. Both adults: pinkish grey faces; *unmarked underparts* buffy cinnamon; red patch on the lower abdomen is often hard to see; wings are finely barred black and creamy white; rump white; pointed tail black and white. Immature: red on nape absent; wings barred ochre and black.

Range. Grand Cayman, Cuba, Bahamas.

Cayman habitat. Breeds and forages in all wooded habitats.

Habits. Drills for ants less than Flicker; also takes fruits, tree

182

frogs and insects (chiefly beetles); it becomes entirely absorbed when foraging, moving round the bole of a tree or on the ground, and can be observed closely. Calls: *key-ou;* and continuous *ke-ke-ke-ke-ke* to its partner. Nests in a cavity drilled in a dead tree, clutch 4, January to August.

Status. Fairly common breeding resident, Grand Cayman only. An endemic subspecies *M. s. caymanensis* (Cory).

YELLOW-BELLIED SAPSUCKER   *Sphyrapicus varius*

Field characters. 20cm:8in Male only: red throat. Female only: white throat. Both adults: red forehead and forecrown; black and white face pattern; back and wings black barred with white; *long white patch on wings shows as white wing coverts in flight at all stages;* black upper breast-band; yellowish underparts, black streaks on sides; white rump; tail black and white with black edges. Immature: brown plumage, unstriped head; black and white on wings and tail.

Range. North America; winters to Greater Antilles and Central America.

Cayman habitat. Inland and coastal woodland; mangrove; trees in disturbed habitat, most easily seen in urban/littoral areas in the southwest Cayman Brac and Little Cayman.

Habits. Drills a series of concentric round holes, sap wells, in the boles of trees (especially palms); silent.

Status. Uncommon to fairly common winter visitor in the three Islands, October to April, the majority from December to February; female and immatures predominate.

NORTHERN FLICKER (Black-heart)   *Colaptes auratus*
Plates 50, 51

Field characters. 33cm:13in *Male only: black malar stripe.* Both adults: cinnamon buff forehead, face, throat and sides of neck; crown and nape grey with a *scarlet triangle on centre nape;* back and wings barred greyish brown and black; *rump white,* *heavily patched with black;* black pointed ragged tail; *large black patch on upper breast; lower breast and abdomen whitish cinnamon with black spots;* in flight under wing-coverts and under tail-coverts are rich yellow. Immature: smaller and paler; malar stripe and chest patch absent.

Range. Grand Cayman, Cuba, North America, Central America.

Cayman habitat. Breeds and forages in all habitats.

Habits. Calls: detected by a staccato *wik-wik-wik-wik* usually answered by a mate; also a single loud *p-e-u* and a soft mumbled *flick-er.* Undulating flight with a golden flash of underwings, landing on sides of trees; feeds almost exclusively on ants, termites and larvae both in trees and on the ground. Nests in tree cavity, January to August.

Status. Fairly common to common breeding resident, Grand Cayman only. An endemic sub-species *C. a. gundlachi* (Cory).

FAMILY TYRANNIDAE: TYRANT FLYCATCHERS.
There are three indigenous species, one summer breeding visitor and four migrants. Dull coloured, mainly insectivorous birds.

CARIBBEAN ELAENIA (Top knot Judas) *Elaenia martinica* **Plates 52, 53, 54**

Field characters. 18cm:7in Breeding: greyish olive upperparts; *white crown patch shows clearly when crest is raised;* two dull whitish wing-bars with pale edges to wing feathers; *bill with pale lower mandible,* often basal part of upper mandible as well; throat, breast and sides greyish white; yellowish wash on abdomen and under tail-coverts. Non-breeding: faded plumage; crown patch not visible; wing-bars buffy; yellowish wash absent. Immature: smaller; indistinct wing-bars; brownish upperparts; greyish buffy underparts; very unlike spring adults.

Range. Cayman Islands, islands off Central America, Puerto Rico south to Trinidad.

Cayman habitat. In all habitats, especially dry and coastal woodland and bushland.

Habits. Territorial; flies very quickly through dense forest in pursuit of an intruder; mostly frugiverous. Immature is especially curious and tame. Open nest, often in bromeliads at low elevations, clutch 2–3 eggs, January to October. Calls: include *ph-eu* rising in centre, *pewit-pewit-pewit,* and variations on *pe-per-wit* repeated.

Status. A very common breeding resident in the three Islands. An endemic sub-species *E. m. caymanensis* (Berlepsch). The only resident flycatcher in Little Cayman.

EASTERN WOOD-PEWEE   *Contopus virens*

Field characters. 16cm:6.25in Dark grey head; yellowish lower mandible; olive grey back; *two very white wing-bars on long olive grey wings,* feathers sharply edged with white; dark tail; whitish throat and abdomen; greyish breast and sides.

Range. North and Central America; winters in South America.

Cayman habitat. Woodland and bushland.

Habits. Calls: *pee-a* (falling)-*wee* and *pee-yyyeer (*falling).

Status. Rare passage migrant, Grand Cayman and Little Cayman, October to April.

LA SAGRA'S FLYCATCHER (Tom Fool)   *Myiarchus sagrae*   **Plates 55, 56**

Field characters. 18.5cm:7.5in. Breeding: clove brown head often with slight crest; heavy black bill, pale at base; back brownish olive; *wings, lower back and rump cinnamon; two white wing-bars* and white edges to wing feathers; long tail with *cinnamon stripes on outer feathers;* throat and breast greyish white; abdomen white; under tail-coverts yellowish; dark legs and feet. Non-breeding: *cinnamon colour becomes worn off feathers leaving grey upperparts and tail.* Immature: very rusty upperparts with greyish underparts. Distinguished from kingbirds by small size and defined wing-bars.

Range. Grand Cayman, Cuba, Bahamas.

Cayman habitat. Mangrove; woodland, bushland and secondary growth.

Habits. Perches low on branches and is very approachable, quiet and inactive; sallies from perch to catch insects, also gleans insects and takes fruits. Calls: rolling *brr-rr* and a single loud *wheet,* together the two vocalizations make up the diagnostic dawn song in the breeding season; continuous alarm call *twe-twe-twe.* Nests in tree holes in Black Mangrove, dead palms and rotted posts, clutch 2–4, April to July.

Status. Fairly common breeding resident, Grand Cayman only. The sub-species *M. s. sagrae* is common to Cuba, Isles of Pines and Grand Cayman.

EASTERN KINGBIRD   *Tyrannus tyrannus*

Field characters. 22cm:8.5in Similar to Loggerhead Kingbird *except head and back are black; black bill is smaller and shorter;* white edges to wing coverts; white underparts with greyish band on breast; *wide white terminal band on unforked black tail.*

Range. North America; winters in southern South America.

Cayman habitat. Urban areas and disturbed woodland and bushland; mangrove.

Status. Uncommon, very occasionally locally fairly common, in passage in the three Islands, mainly in fall, September to April.

GRAY KINGBIRD   *Tyrannus dominicensis*
  Plate 57

Field characters. 23cm:9.25in *Pale grey head and back,* orange crown patch seldom visible in the field; *black band from man-dibles under eye to ear coverts;* dark grey wings with pale edges to coverts; whitish grey underparts; large heavy black bill with bristles at base; *tail notched.*

Range. Cayman Islands, West Indies, southeastern United States to northern South America; North American and some Greater Antillean birds winter in South America.

Cayman habitat. Prefers more open habitats than Logger-head: inland and coastal dry open bushland; disturbed habitats including urban areas.

Habits. Perches on wires and emergent trees to take prey on the wing; also eats fruits. Very vocal, call: sharp *pi-tirr-re,* song: 6 syllable variation on call. Arrives in large flocks; in Little Cayman and Cayman Brac after establishing breeding territories it becomes aggressive and highly territorial; clutch 2–4, in loose nest, May-September with peaks June and July. Shows flocking behaviour throughout the summer, Grand Cayman.

Status. Common summer breeding visitor, Cayman Brac and Little Cayman; reports of occasional juveniles but status is of a non-breeding summer visitor, Grand Cayman; March to November, majority depart in October.

LOGGERHEAD KINGBIRD (Tom Fighter)   *Tyrannus caudifasciatus*   **Plates 58, 59**

Field characters. 23.5cm:9.25in Adult: dark greyish clove brown head with yellow crown patch concealed; *long, heavy flattened black bill* with bristles at base; *olive brown back and darker wings;* coverts edged whitish, may form two indistinct wing-bars; *square tail with whitish terminal band;* rufous upper tail-coverts; underparts whitish to pure white with yellowish wash on sides and abdomen; yellow edge of wing, under wing- and under tail-coverts. Immature: greyish brown upperparts; rufous edges to wing coverts; whitish edges to wing feathers and tail band; underparts white.

Range. Cayman Islands, Greater Antilles, Bahamas.

Cayman habitat. In all habitats, Grand Cayman; the edge of bluff woodland and, uncommonly, on the northern coastal plain, Cayman Brac.

Habits. Grand Cayman: highly territorial and visible in the breeding season; raises crest and attacks intruders with loud aggressive calls. Commonly seen perched on exposed posts, tree branches and wires to take prey in the air, returning to perch to beat it before swallowing; also takes prey on the ground and gleans insects in branches. Flies in a swoop with wings held closed between beats, alighting on the upward arc. Cayman Brac: shy and much less visible though behaviour similar. Calls: *pee pee uuup*, alarm *pe-pe-pe-pe*, song: 4 syllables (rising) and a short series. Loosely woven nest in outer branch of a tree, clutch 2–4, February to August.

Status. Common breeding resident, Grand Cayman, uncommon, Cayman Brac; extirpated, Little Cayman though small flocks have been reported briefly in spring since the 1988 hurricane. An endemic subspecies *T. c. caymanensis* (Nicoll).

FAMILY HIRUNDINIDAE: SWALLOWS. All members of this group are passage migrants. In flight, the shape of the tail and colour of the rump are helpful field points.

PURPLE MARTIN   *Progne subis*

Field characters. 19cm:7.5in Large. Male: *entirely steely blue black plumage;* forked tail. Female: dull grey brown and purple upperparts, grey forehead with blue on ear-coverts; throat, *breast and sides are grey, checkered with brown;* abdomen greyish white; pale edges to wing 'wrist' when perched. Immature male: similar to female but paler with greyish underparts. Females and immatures predominate.

Range. North America and Mexico; winters to South America.

Habits. Gregarious, usually in large noisy flocks; flapping flight with bursts of gliding in circles and spirals; takes beetles, ants, wasps, butterflies and dragonflies on the wing.

Status. Passage migrant in the three Islands, locally common in fall, July to October, and uncommon in spring, March to May; flocks may remain for several weeks, usually in urban areas or near the coast.

CARIBBEAN MARTIN   *Progne dominicensis*

Field characters. 17 cm:7in Male: glossy steel blue upperparts, throat and breast; *white lower breast, abdomen and under tail-coverts.* Female: similar to Purple Martin except for darker breast and whiter abdomen.

Range. West Indies and Mexico.

Status. Very rare passage migrant in spring. A new species, previously considered a sub-species of the Purple Martin (*P. subis*), its taxonomy is still unclear (AOU 1983); Cayman records may be of the Cuban species, *P. cryptoleuca.*

TREE SWALLOW   *Tachycineta bicolor*

Field characters. 14cm:5.5in Chunky shape; broad wing forms a triangle. Male: dark metallic blue green upperparts and head to below eye; *entirely white underparts extending to sides of dark rump in a notch;* pale under wing-coverts; *slightly forked tail.* Female: similar but duller. Immature female only: greyish brown becoming blue green in second year. Immature: brown upperparts, tertials tipped white; whitish underparts with an indistinct breast band allows confusion with Bank and Rough-winged Swallows.

Range. North America; winters to southern United States, Greater Antilles and Central America.

Habits. Rapid direct flight interspersed with long glides; often with other swallows along coasts and over grassland.

Status. Locally common passage migrant in the three Islands, mainly January to April, rare in fall, September to May.

NORTHERN ROUGH-WINGED SWALLOW
Stelgidopteryx serripennis

Field characters. 14cm:5.5in Long wings. Completely brownish grey upperparts; *pale rump; grey brown throat, upper breast and sides*, rest of underparts white; tail more square than forked. Juvenile: cinnamon wash overall.

Range. North and Central America; migrates through the Bahamas and Greater Antilles to Mexico and Central America.

Habits. Often with Barn Swallows over open ground, ponds, shores and airports; similar strong straight flight with a suggestions of a pause after each deep slow wing stroke.

Status. Fairly common in passage in the three Islands, August to May. Main peaks August to November with smaller peaks from March to April; uncommon from mid-December to February, and May.

BANK SWALLOW   *Riparia riparia*

Field characters. 12.5cm:5in Similar but slightly smaller than Northern Rough-winged Swallow; darker brown upperparts, *may show a pale rump;* throat and underparts white except for contrasting *brown band across upper breast; squarish tail, very slightly forked.* Juvenile: pale edges to wing feathers; buffy rump.

Range. North America; winters in South America. Cosmopolitan.

Habits. Fluttering flight to the top of an arc, frequent glides followed by shallow fast wing strokes.

190

Status. Uncommon to locally common passage migrant in the three Islands, main peaks August to November with smaller peaks from March to May; uncommon, December to February.

CLIFF SWALLOW   *Hirundo pyrrhonota*

Field characters. 14.0cm:5.5in Adult: metallic blue wings and crown; white streaks on back; *pale forehead;* grey hindneck; *chestnut face and throat* with black border patch to upper breast; whitish grey underparts; *square tail; chestnut rump appears pale in flight,* contrasts with dark back and tail.

Range. North America and Mexico; winters in South America.

Status. Very uncommon spring passage migrant, February to May, rare in fall; usually with Barn Swallows.

CAVE SWALLOW   *Hirundo fulva*

Field characters. 12.5cm:5in Similar to Cliff Swallow *except forehead is chestnut not pale;* chin, throat and collar are pale to dark cinnamon; cinnamon streaks on sides; chestnut rump.

Range. Limited range in North America to South America and the Greater Antilles; much of the population is sedentary except that of Cuba.

Status. Rare in passage in the three Islands, September to October and February to March. Bond records that October records may be Cuban migrants.

BARN SWALLOW   *Hirundo rustica*

Field characters. 18cm:7in Adult: glossy dark blue upperparts and rump; *chestnut forehead, chin and throat, separated from the cinnamon breast and abdomen by partial dark collar; swallow-tailed with white tailspots.* Immature: creamy forehead; shorter forked tail *with tail spots;* throat dark cinnamon to rufous, streaked with black which may continue down the sides; breast pale washed cinnamon to whitish on abdomen. Adults arrive before immatures in fall.

Range. North America and Mexico; winters from Puerto Rico south through the Lesser Antilles to South America. Cosmopolitan.

Habits. Calls: twittering and a single *twit* repeated. Wings swept back and almost closed between wing beats, fast low zig-zagging flight over land and water in open and coastal habitats.

Status. Common to abundant passage migrant in the three Islands, August to November and March to May; uncommon in winter. Migrant flocks numbering many thousand are occasionally brought down by storms.

FAMILY MUSCICAPIDAE: OLD WORLD WAR-BLERS AND THRUSHES. The only endemic species, the Grand Cayman Thrush, is now regarded as extinct; there is one endemic sub-species. Three migrants have been recorded.

BLUE-GRAY GNATCATCHER   *Polioptila caerulea*

Field characters. 11cm:4.5in A tiny wren-like bird; dark wings; underparts whitish; *long black tail with white edges; white eye-ring.* Male only: black stripe across forehead and over eye to ear coverts; blue grey upperparts. Female and immature: black on face absent; upperparts grey.

Range. Southern North America to Central America and the Bahamas. North American birds winter to the Bahamas, Cuba and the Cayman Islands.

Cayman habitat. Mangrove; woodland and bushland.

Habits. Flits among branches like a butterfly; sits with wings drooped and tail erect like a mini-Mockingbird. Call: nasal *zzpee,* repeated.

Status. Uncommon winter visitor in the three Islands, August to April.

VEERY *Catharus fuscescens*

Field characters. 18cm:7.5in *Cinnamon brown upperparts;* lore to eye pale; indistinct eye-ring; ear coverts brownish; *cinnamon buff wash on lightly spotted breast;* grey sides; rest of underparts whitish.

Range. North America; winters in South America.

Status. Very rare passage migrant in the three Islands, September and October, April and May.

The two following species, one very rare the other unconfirmed, are included to allow descriptive comparison among similar species of migrant thrushes.

GRAY-CHEEKED THRUSH *Catharus minimus*

Field characters. 18cm:7.5in Grey brown upperparts; *grey cheeks and ear coverts; underparts white, throat streaked and breast heavily spotted blackish;* sides and flanks brownish.

Range. North America; winters in South America.

Status. No confirmed records; several unconfirmed reports.

SWAINSON'S THRUSH *Catharus ustulatus*

Field characters. 18cm:7.5in Olive brown upperparts; *buff lores, eye-ring and ear coverts; buffy cinnamon upper breast with dark brown spotting;* sides and flanks brownish grey.

Range. North America; winters in Central and South America.

Status. Uncommon to rare in passage, September to November.

GRAND CAYMAN THRUSH   *Turdus ravidus*

Field characters. 27cm:11in Ashy grey plumage except for white lower abdomen and under tail-coverts; three outer tail feathers white tipped; eye-ring, bill and feet coral red.

Status. Extinct. Previously Grand Cayman only. The only species, as opposed to sub-species, endemic to the Cayman Islands; not recorded since 1938. It inhabited dense forest in the north and east of Grand Cayman. Formerly called *Mimocichla ravida*.

RED-LEGGED THRUSH (Old Thruss)   *Turdus plumbeus*
Plate 60

Field characters. 26cm:10.5in Large grey thrush. Adult: *slate grey body darker on upperparts;* wings black with white edges to flight feathers and grey coverts; blackish lores; white chin immaculate or crossed by fine black lines extending as *white malar stripe;* black throat; *red eye-ring;* bill red, black distally; *legs coral red; lower abdomen to vent has various amounts of blackish orange to a rich cinnamon orange;* white under tail-coverts; long black tail, white spots underneath show as white edges to outer feathers in flight.

Range. Cayman Islands, Greater Antilles (absent Jamaica) and the Bahamas.

Cayman habitat. Coastal woodland and bushland; bluff woodland; urban areas.

Habits. Breeding, March to September: observed throughout, chiefly along the northern coastal plain and the bluff, becoming highly territorial and aggressive. October to February: rarely observed, confined to bluff woodland, silent and shy. Song: loud musical and assertive, single phrases with a pause between, many variations include *pzzurt tzzeet* (emphatic) *ptururp tzza pheuu tzzt* often followed by a bell-like trill. Calls: *treer*, and *pzt pzt pzt*, repeated. Large open nests from 6 to 20 feet elevation in the bushes and trees, or around dwellings often in the water piping surrounding the roof, clutch 3–4, March to July. The thrush is continually threatened by Mockingbirds.

Status. Common breeding resident, Cayman Brac only. An endemic subspecies, *T. p. coryi* (Sharpe).

FAMILY MIMIDAE: MIMIC-THRUSHES. Throughout the Americas; one resident and one migrant occur in the Islands. Sexes alike.

GRAY CATBIRD   *Dumetella carolinensis*

Field characters. 23cm:9in Grey plumage, dark slate on upperparts; *black forehead and crown;* long black tail; *orange brown under tail-coverts;* paler grey underparts.

Range. North America; winters in the breeding range, the western Greater Antilles, Central and South America.

Cayman habitat. Woodland and bushland; mangrove; Logwood, Grand Cayman.

Habits. Shy but inquisitive, seldom emerges but calls frequently from cover, call: cat-like *m-e-a;* flicks tail and holds it erect with wings drooped.

Status. Fairly common winter visitor in the three Islands, September to May, becoming common in some years.

NORTHERN MOCKINGBIRD (Nightingale)   *Mimus polyglottos*   **Plate 61**

Field characters. 25cm:10in. Grey and white. Adult: upperparts pale grey; *dark grey wings broadly edged with white,*

white patch on edge of closed wing; whitish grey underparts; grey eye-line; pale iris; tail black, white underneath shows as white outer tail feathers in flight. Plumage become brighter in breeding season. Immature: brownish grey upperparts; buffy underparts.

Range. Cayman Islands, Bahamas and Greater Antilles, North America and Mexico.

Cayman habitat. Disturbed habitat including urban/littoral areas; dry bushland.

Habits. Perches on an emergent branch to sing beautiful elaborate liquid songs: 8–10 phrases (including *peter*) repeated two or three times, often mimicking other species; Calls: loud alarm *check* and a growling *churr*. Feeds on the ground, alights with long tail held vertically and wings drooped; opens and closes raised wings to display diagnostic dark grey and white wing pattern, called wing-flashing. Swooping flight. Rough open nest in trees and bushes, often two clutches of 3–4, December to August.

Status. Very common breeding resident, Grand Cayman; common, Cayman Brac and Little Cayman. Populations are increasing in the three Islands.

FAMILY BOMBYCILLIDAE: WAXWINGS.

CEDAR WAXWING   *Bombycilla cedrorum*

Field characters. 18cm:7in Brownish upperparts; *head conspicuously crested;* grey wings; *broad black eye-line;* black bill and chin; brown breast; yellowish abdomen; white under tail-coverts; *grey tail broadly tipped yellow.*

Range. North America; winters to northern South America.

Status. Rare spring migrant in the three Islands, February to May, though flocks in excess of a hundred birds may occur. This species is increasing its winter range in the West Indies.

196

FAMILY VIREONIDAE: VIREOS. Dull plumaged birds, best identified by song. Three species breed and three species are regular migrants. The Yucatan Vireo, an endemic subspecies, is only found along parts of the coast of Central America and in Grand Cayman.

WHITE-EYED VIREO   *Vireo griseus*

Field characters. 12.5cm:5in Greyish head, greyish olive neck and back; *eye has white iris; whitish throat and underparts and yellow sides* distinguish it from the Thick-billed Vireo, which has entirely yellow underparts. Yellow across forehead *continues around eyes; dark line from bill to eye; two whitish wing-bars.*

Range. Eastern North America to Mexico; winters to the Greater Antilles, the Bahamas and Central America.

Cayman habitat. Woodland and secondary bushland; mangrove.

Habits. Loud song: 5–7 syllable *chip-a-tee-weeo-chic* with variations; call: *pick* similar to Thick-billed Vireo. Very curious and approachable, usually perches at low elevations.

Status. Uncommon winter visitor in the three Islands, September to April; locally fairly common when arriving in Grand Cayman in fall.

THICK-BILLED VIREO (Shear-bark)   *Vireo crassirostris*
Plate 62

Field characters. 13cm:5in Adult: crown grey; back and wings olive green; *two whitish to white wing-bars;* whitish edges to wing feathers; thick, slightly hooked bill; *bright yellow across forehead continuing around eyes as 'spectacles'; line from eye to base of bill is more pronounced than White-eyed Vireo; underparts entirely buffy yellow to yellowish;* under tail-coverts yellow. Immature: olive upperparts and olive-yellow underparts; dark line to bill faint. Adult plumage becomes faded in winter.

Range. Cayman Islands, the Bahamas, an island off Hispaniola and two islands off the coast of Central America.

Cayman habitat. Open woodland and bushland; mangrove; urban areas in Cayman Brac.

Habits. Curious and tame; creeps among branches looking for insects and berries. Easily detected from February to July when it perches on exposed branches. Song: loud, and assertive with many variations, usually ending in *chik*, e.g., *per-wee didle wer chik,* repeated. Breeds April to July, clutch of 2, in delicate round cup nest suspended between a branch fork.

Status. A fairly common to common breeding resident, Grand Cayman and Cayman Brac; extirpated, Little Cayman. An endemic sub-species *V. c. alleni* (Cory).

YELLOW-THROATED VIREO   *Vireo flavifrons*

Field characters. 14cm:5.5in Crown olive; upperparts greenish; *throat and breast yellow; abdomen white; two sharply defined white wing-bars;* grey rump. Face with 'spectacles' similar to Thick-billed Vireo except *loral line less pronounced; eye dark.*

Range. Eastern North America; winters to western Greater Antilles, Central America and northern South America.

Cayman habitat. Urban/ littoral areas; mangrove.

Habits. Song: 2–3 note phrases repeated, *wee-ar-ee whu ar.*

Status. Very uncommon winter visitor in the three Islands, September to March.

RED-EYED VIREO   *Vireo olivaceus*

Field characters. 15cm:6in *Wing bars absent;* very similar to Black-whiskered Vireo, *except malar stripe absent;* superciliary stripe and underparts *white;* shorter and finer bill; red iris. Immature: iris brown.

Range. North America; winters in South America.

Status. Very uncommon passage migrant mainly in urban/littoral habitats, September-early November; records for Grand Cayman only.

BLACK-WHISKERED VIREO   *Vireo altiloquus*
Plate 63

Field characters. 16.5cm:6.5in Adult: *crown grey bordered by blackish lateral stripes;* buffy white superciliary stripe; black eye-line; *black malar stripe;* upperparts brownish olive grey; *no wing-bars;* ivory throat and underparts; yellowish sides and under tail-coverts; thick bill; red iris.

Range. Cayman Islands, Greater Antilles, the Bahamas and Florida Keys; winters in South America, rarely in the West Indies.

Cayman habitat. In the canopy of mature woodland.

Habits. Song: loud clear continuous single and double couplets *good-john to-whit,* also *chew-we.* Nest similar to Thick-billed Vireo, clutch 3 reported, June and July. Gleans insects from canopy foliage.

Status. Fairly common summer breeding visitor, February (mainly March) to September, in its restricted habitat, Cayman Brac and Little Cayman; in passage, Grand Cayman, non-breeding.

YUCATAN VIREO (Sweet Bridget)   *Vireo magister*
Plates 64, 65

Field characters. 15cm:6in Breeding: olive grey upperparts, crown brownish olive, *crown and upperparts appear similar in colour in the field;* wings dull brown edged with olive, wingbars absent; rump and upper tail-coverts bright olive; whitish superciliary stripe; *broad slate line through eye to ear coverts* and buffy cheeks; lower mandible pale; underparts greyish white with pronounced yellowish wash from abdomen to under tail-coverts; tail olive brown with greenish edges. Non-breeding: becomes nondescript and dull; buffy grey superciliary; eye-line grey; underparts pinkish buff. Similar to Black-whiskered Vireo and Red-eyed Vireo except *malar stripe and crown stripe absent; little contrast between crown and back.*

Range. Grand Cayman and coastal Central America.

Cayman habitat. Mangrove; woodland especially in winter; Logwood.

Habits. Shy; quietly creeping among the leaves, blending perfectly with its surroundings. Feeds mostly on fruits. Best located by distinctive song: 2 syllable whistle *whoi whu*, and three syllable *sweet brid-get*. Deep cup nest, clutch of 2, woven into the fork of a branch, April to August.

Status. Fairly common breeding resident, Grand Cayman only. An endemic sub-species: *V. m. caymanensis* (Cory).

FAMILY EMBERIZIDAE:
SUB-FAMILY PARULINAE, WOOD WARBLERS.

The great majority of this large sub-family are migrants; only two species breed, the Vitelline Warbler (*Dendroica vitellina*) and the Yellow Warbler (*Dendroica petechia*). Warblers are difficult to identify in fall and early winter as the majority are immatures or adult females assuming their drab winter coat. By late December to mid-January most adults resume full breeding plumage and the males are brightly coloured. Migrant Warblers predominate in mangrove, urban/littoral areas (especially gardens close to the shore) and woodland. For identification, two important points to notice are the presence or absence of wing-bars and the superciliary stripe. Late September to early October is the peak arrival time, though a few species e.g. Prairie Warbler are earlier. The majority have departed by late April.

BLUE-WINGED WARBLER   *Vermivora pinus*

Field characters. 13cm:5in Breeding male: *golden yellow head and underparts*. Breeding female and immature: crown greenish; yellow of underparts less golden. All: *slender bill; black eye-line;* greenish nape and mantle; *two white wing-bars* on blue grey wings; white under tail-coverts.

Range. Eastern United States; winters in Central America.

Status. Rare winter visitor and passage migrant, September to March, mainly in fall.

GOLDEN-WINGED WARBLER *Vermivora chrysoptera*

Field characters. 12cm:4.75in Breeding male: *golden crown and patch on wing coverts;* upperparts slate blue; *black patch over eye to ear coverts;* white malar and superciliary stripes; *chin to upper breast black;* whitish underparts. Breeding female: duller; predominantly grey, *dark grey on face and throat;* brownish crown; yellow wing coverts.

Range. Southeastern North America; winters to Central America and northern South America, rarely to the West Indies.

Status. Rare passage migrant, mainly September and October.

TENNESSEE WARBLER *Vermivora peregrina*

Field characters. 11cm:4.5in *Back grass-green* in all plumages; dark eye-line; fine straight bill; short tail; *white under tail-coverts.* Breeding male: grey head and cheeks; *white superciliary stripe;* white underparts. Breeding female breeding, non-breeding adults and immature: crown olive green; *yellowish superciliary stripe;* yellowish wash on breast and sides; (immature only has yellowish wash on entire underparts and a single faint wing-bar).

Range. Northern North America; winters to Central America and northern South America.

Cayman habitat. Disturbed bushland; secondary mangrove.

Status. Uncommon to locally fairly common passage migrant in the three Islands, September to April, mainly September to November; rare in winter and very uncommon in spring.

NASHVILLE WARBLER *Vermivora ruficapilla*

Field characters. 12cm:4.75in Male: grey head. Female: olive head. Both: olive green upperparts; unmarked wings;

white eye-ring; yellow underparts except for whitish lower abdomen. Immature: similar except upperparts brownish.

Range. North America; winters in Central America, rarely in the West Indies.

Status. Rare passage and winter migrant, mainly September to February.

NORTHERN PARULA   *Parula americana*

Field characters. 11cm:4.5in Small. Adult and immature: blue grey upperparts, *greenish on mantle; broken white eye-ring; two broad white wing-bars;* yellow throat and breast; rest of underparts white. Breeding male: plumage brighter; *chestnut and blue grey necklace across breast.*

Range. Eastern North America; winters in the breeding range, West Indies and Central America.

Cayman habitat. Mangrove; woodland and bushland; urban/littoral areas.

Habits. Forages at all elevations including the canopy of tall trees. Call: *teip;* song: continuous *zze-zee-zee-zee* (rising)-*ip.*

Status. Fairly common winter visitor in the three Islands, September to April.

YELLOW WARBLER (Yellow Bird)   *Dendroica petechia*
Plate 66

Field characters. 13cm:5.5in Breeding male: *brilliant rufous crown* cap; streaking brighter. Non-breeding male: bright yellow forehead, face, crown and underparts; upperparts greenish yellow; *chestnut streaking on yellow breast.* Breeding female: duller, upperparts olive green; faint streaks on breast; pale yellow underparts. Both adults: slender dark bill; black eye; *two yellow wing-bars and yellow tail spots.* Immature: *greyish crown and hindneck;* sides of head and neck dull brownish grey; buffy olive upperparts, becoming greenish on mantle and wings; white throat and upper breast; lower breast and abdomen whitish buff; sides and flanks yellowish olive; *pale yellow under tail-coverts and tail spots;* very dissimilar to adult.

Range. Cayman Islands, West Indies and North and Central America; North American birds winter to the West Indies and South America.

Cayman habitat. Chiefly in mangrove and Buttonwood swamps; littoral and inland woodland; Logwood, Grand Cayman.

Habits. Song: varied, 6–10 syllable *tse-tse-tse-tsu-tsuta-tstste-tse* (rising); call: *chip* and *peet*. Small cup nest woven in a branch fork from 4 to 20 feet elevation, clutch 2 to 3, March to August.

Status. Common breeding resident, Grand Cayman and Little Cayman; uncommon, Cayman Brac. North American migrants occur in winter, September to March (Bond).

CHESTNUT-SIDED WARBLER   *Dendroica pensylvanica*

Field characters. 13cm:5in Breeding male: *yellow crown; broad black eye-line and long malar stripe* continuous with *chestnut sides and flanks; upperparts yellowish green strongly streaked black;* two yellowish wing-bars; sides of neck and underparts white. Breeding female: crown duller; chestnut reduced on sides. Non-breeding and immature: *crown and back bright lime green; white eye-ring;* dark wings with *yellow wing-bars;* face and sides greyish (chestnut usually absent); rest of underparts whitish.

Range. Eastern North America; winters in Central America.

Cayman habitat. Urban areas; bushland.

Status. Rare passage migrant in the three Islands, though numbers seem to be increasing; mainly September and October, also February to May.

MAGNOLIA WARBLER *Dendroica magnolia*

Field characters. 12cm:4.75in All plumages: grey crown; yellow underparts and rump; white under tail-coverts; *black tail with white band across complete underside and on outer thirds of uppertail* diagnostic at all stages. Breeding male: *black band from forehead to ear coverts; white superciliary from eye to ear coverts;* black back; *white wing covert patch;* bold black streaks on sides join black breast-band. Breeding female: two white wing-bars; olive grey back with black streaks; reduced black streaking on sides and flanks. Non-breeding adults and immature: male resembles female; upperparts greenish streaked with black; faint superciliary stripe; two white wing-bars; streaking on sides darkest in male, faintest in immature.

Range. North America; winters in southern United States, Greater Antilles, Bahamas and Central America.

Cayman habitat. Mangrove; woodland; urban/littoral areas.

Status. Uncommon passage migrant and rare winter visitor in the three Islands, August to May.

CAPE MAY WARBLER *Dendroica tigrina*

Field characters. 13cm:5.0in Breeding male: blackish crown; greenish back heavily streaked with black; *large white wing patch; orange yellow superciliary and sides of neck; chestnut ear coverts;* yellow underparts with heavy black streaks; white under tail-coverts; yellow rump. Breeding female: yellow on neck duller; *ear coverts grey;* blackish streaks on yellowish underparts; two white wing-bars. Non-breeding: male resembles female but retains white wing patch and shows more yellow on underparts. Immature: grey face and ear coverts; *yellowish neck patch; buffy yellow superciliary stripe; yellowish rump;* underparts yellowish with dusky streaks; two faint white wing-bars.

Range. North America; winters in mainly in the West Indies and Florida.

Cayman habitat. Prefers altered habitats: edges of second growth bushland; urban areas; open woodland.

Habits. Often in small flocks; call: weak and high-pitched *see*, repeated.

Status. Fairly common to locally common winter visitor, Grand Cayman and Cayman Brac; uncommon, Little Cayman. Mainly October to April.

BLACK-THROATED BLUE WARBLER   *Dendroica caerulescens*

Field characters. 13cm:5in Breeding male: grey blue upperparts; *black forehead, face, throat and sides;* white underparts; white on outer tail. *White rectangle on centre edge of closed wing* diagnostic in all plumages and both sexes (may be absent in some immatures). Breeding female and immature: olive replaces blue on upperparts; pale superciliary stripe; grey face; underparts buffy.

Range. Eastern North America; winters in Greater Antilles, Bahamas, Florida, and rarely to Central and northern South America.

Cayman habitat. Mangrove; littoral and inland woodland and bushland; urban areas.

Status. Fairly common winter visitor in the three Islands, September to May.

YELLOW-RUMPED WARBLER   *Dendroica coronata*

Field characters. 14cm:5.5in All adults: *bright yellow rump; white throat, superciliary stripe,* abdomen and under tail-coverts; two white wing-bars; *yellow patch on crown (reduced in female) and sides.* Breeding male: dark grey upperparts streaked with black; black forehead and face patch; lower eye-ring white; black breast-band and streaks on sides. Breeding female: similar but duller; blackish streaking on breast. Non-breeding: brownish upperparts, streaked; buffy white breast is streaked brown, faint yellow on sides. Immature: similar except *dark face, superciliary absent; yellow on sides and streaking on breast may be absent, may show yellow on rump only.*

Range. Northern North America; winters in North America, West Indies and Central America.

Cayman habitat. Littoral and inland woodland and bushland; urban areas and secondary growth.

Habits. Call: a loud *chek.*

Status. Winter visitor, varies from rare to locally common in some years in the three Islands, mainly October to April.

BLACK-THROATED GREEN WARBLER   *Dendroica virens*

Field characters. 13cm:5in Breeding male: *black throat and upper breast;* bold black streaks on sides and flanks. Breeding female: pale throat; blackish breast and less streaking on sides. Both adults and immature: olive green upperparts; dark wings with two broad white wing-bars; *yellow superciliary stripe and face with dark eye-line and ear coverts;* white abdomen and yellowish under tail-coverts. Non-breeding female and immature: similar except olive brown face; buffy whitish underparts faintly streaked on sides only.

Range. North America; winters in the Greater Antilles, Central America to Panama.

Cayman habitat. In all habitats.

Status. Very uncommon to rare winter visitor in the three Islands, mainly October to March.

BLACKBURNIAN WARBLER   *Dendroica fusca*

Field characters. 13cm:5.0in Breeding male: *orange yellow crown, face and sides of neck join orange throat and upper breast;* black hind-crown, nape, eye-line and ear coverts; back striped with black and white; *large white patch on wing and outer tail feathers;* abdomen and under tail-coverts white; black streaks on sides. Non-breeding male, breeding female and immature male: duller; upperparts greyish with black streaks; ear coverts blackish brown; various amounts of yellow on crown, super-ciliary, *throat and breast;* streaking on sides lighter; two white wing-bars. Non-breeding female and immature: similar except crown olive grey; underparts buffy (throat may show yellow wash), olive streaks on sides.

Range. Eastern North America; winters to Central and South America.

Cayman habitat. Canopy of tall trees, including coastal littoral.

Status. Very uncommon passage migrant in the three Islands, mainly February to May, also September and October.

YELLOW-THROATED WARBLER *Dendroica dominica*

Field characters. 13cm:5.0in Sexes alike. Adult: grey crown and upperparts; two white wing-bars; *black face; white superciliary joins white sides of neck;* lower eye-ring white; black continues down sides of *bright lemon yellow throat and upper breast* to black streaking on sides; white breast and abdomen. In contrast, the Kentucky Warbler has superciliary stripe and all underparts yellow.

Range. Southeastern United States and Bahamas; winters in the breeding range, the Greater Antilles and Central America.

Cayman habitat. Mangrove including Buttonwood and secondary swamp; urban/littoral areas.

Status. Fairly common winter visitor, Grand Cayman and Little Cayman; uncommon, Cayman Brac; July to April.

PINE WARBLER *Dendroica pinus*

Field characters. 14cm:5.5in Breeding male: unmarked greenish olive upperparts; dark wings, *two white wing-bars;* yellowish superciliary; throat and *breast yellow,* sides of breast streaked; abdomen and under tail-coverts white. Breeding female and non-breeding adults are duller. Immature male:

brownish-olive upperparts; buffy white wing-bars; buffy yellow anterior underparts with brownish streaks on flanks; female similar except underparts whitish, sides and flanks buff.

Range. Eastern United States and the Bahamas; winters in the breeding range and to Hispaniola.

Status. Casual, very rare, October records for Grand Cayman only. Casual in Cuba, 22 October-8 November (Bond).

PRAIRIE WARBLER   *Dendroica discolor*

Field characters. 12cm:4.75in Breeding male: olive green upperparts and rump; chestnut streaks on back; *two yellowish wing-bars* (often appears either as one yellow wing covert patch or the lower bar is indistinct); *black eye-line; black malar stripe curves below eye; yellow below eye; superciliary stripe and entire underparts yellow; heavy black streaking on sides of neck and breast to flanks;* white on outer tail feathers. Breeding female and non-breeding adults: streaking reduced on back and sides; face markings paler; yellow duller. Immature: head greyish; whitish superciliary and throat; faint streaks on sides.

Range. Eastern United States; winters in southern breeding range, Bahamas, West Indies and islands off Central America.

Cayman habitat. In all habitats, second growth areas preferred.

Habits. Call: *chit;* song: *zee-zee-zee,* repeated up to fifteen times and rising. Slim outline, very active and bobs its tail.

Status. Fairly common winter visitor and passage migrant in the three Islands, August to May, with a few birds in June and July.

VITELLINE WARBLER (Chip Chip)   *Dendroica vitellina*
Plates 67, 68, 69

Field characters. 13cm:5.0in Adult is larger and more yellow than immature Prairie Warbler. Grand Cayman sub-

208

species, male: lemon yellow forehead and long superciliary; *greyish olive eye-line and malar stripe which curves below eye to olive grey ear coverts*, enclosing a yellow area below eye; upperparts greenish yellow; two lemon yellow wing-bars, the second often indistinct or darker yellow; may have olive grey patch on lower neck; white spots on outer tail; pale yellowish green or olive edges to slate wing and tail feathers; *yellow underparts, obscure greyish olive streaking on sides and flanks*. Female: duller; olive head; ear coverts yellow; streaking very faint or absent. Immature: olive grey upperparts; eye-line, malar stripe, streaking on sides and wing-bars all faint to absent; pale buff superciliary and forehead; underparts whitish to yellowish buff. Juvenile: greyish upperparts; buffy wingbars; whitish yellow lower abdomen and under tail-coverts. Cayman Brac and Little Cayman sub-species: slightly larger; appears more yellow as eye-line and malar stripe show less contrast; face and superciliary intense yellow; upperparts yellow; underparts chrome yellow.

Range. Cayman Islands and Swan Island.

Cayman habitat. Dry bushland and woodland; disturbed habitats including urban areas; Logwood, Grand Cayman; usually absent from mangrove and littoral habitats, though occasionally nests in mixed Logwood/Buttonwood, Grand Cayman and urban/littoral areas throughout.

Habits. Curious and tame. Very active when gleaning insects foraging from the ground to the canopy of tall trees; also takes fruits and nectar. Male flicks and fans tail during courtship. Song: distinctive 3, 4 or 5 syllable *tswee tswee tswee* (rising) *tse*, slightly grating; call: *chip*, repeated. Small cup nest lined with feathers woven in uprights of a fine branch or bush, usually between 3 to 10 feet elevation, clutch of 2, April to early August.

Status. A breeding resident in the three Islands. Two endemic sub-species: *D. v. vitellina* (Cory) is common in Grand Cayman; *D. v. crawfordi* (Nicoll) is very common in Cayman Brac and Little Cayman.

WOOD WARBLERS

PALM WARBLER *Dendroica palmarum*

Field characters. 13cm:5in Breeding adult: *chestnut crown;* greyish brown sides of neck, ear coverts and streaked upperparts; yellowish rump; yellow superciliary stripe; black eyeline; bright yellow throat and upper breast with fine rufous streaks; abdomen buffy; *under tail-coverts yellow in all plumages.* Immature and non-breeding adult: upperparts brownish grey; underparts buffy grey with less streaking; *white superciliary stripe.*

Range. North America; winters in southern United States, Bahamas, the Greater Antilles and Central America.

Cayman habitat. Prefers disturbed open habitats, but occurs in all habitats except dense woodland and mangrove.

Habits. Forages on the ground, in low bushes and grassland; constantly flicks tail. Call: *chit,* sharp; song: *zee zee zee zee zee zee,* fluid.

Status. Common to abundant winter visitor in the three Islands, September to May, peak arrivals in October and peak departures in April.

BAY-BREASTED WARBLER *Dendroica castanea*

Field characters. 14cm:5.5in Breeding male: black forehead and face; grey upperparts streaked with black; *chestnut crown, throat, sides of breast and sides; buffy patch on sides of neck;* rest of underparts whitish. All plumages: *two white wing-bars;* streaked back; dark legs and feet. Breeding female: grey crown; no black on face; dark ear coverts; chestnut reduced to pale wash on hind crown and sides and flanks. Non-breeding adults and immature: greenish upperparts with faint black streaks; *buffy underparts (including under tail-coverts)* with chestnut on sides of male only. Similar immatures: Blackpoll Warbler has white under tail-coverts; Pine Warbler has buffy wing-bars.

Range. North America; winters to Panama, Trinidad and northern South America.

Status. Very uncommon passage migrant, mainly April and May, also October and November.

BLACKPOLL WARBLER   *Dendroica striata*

Field characters. 14cm:5.5in Breeding male: *black forehead and crown to eye; white cheeks;* black throat; brownish grey upperparts streaked with black; *underparts white with black streaks from neck to flanks.* Female: *crown and upperparts olive grey* with dark streaks; *pale superciliary;* grey eye-line; grey streaking on yellowish green underparts. Non-breeding adults and immature: greenish olive upperparts streaked; underparts yellowish, faint streaking on sides. All: two white wing-bars; *the majority have pale legs and feet; white under tail-coverts.*

Range. Northern North America; winters in South America.

Cayman habitat. Woodland; mangrove; urban/littoral areas.

Status. Uncommon but regular passage migrant in the three Islands, mainly April and May, also September and October.

CERULEAN WARBLER   *Dendroica cerulea*

Field characters. 11cm:4.5in Breeding male: *head and upperparts bright blue;* dark eye-line; white underparts with narrow black breast-band and black streaks on sides. Breeding female and immature male: blue grey head; greenish grey upperparts; pale superciliary stripe; yellow wash on whitish underparts, pale streaking on sides. Immature female: greenish or brownish upperparts; yellowish underparts. All: two white wing-bars.

Range. Eastern United States; winters in South America.

Status. Very rare passage migrant in fall and spring (in April), records for Grand Cayman only.

BLACK-AND-WHITE WARBLER *Mniotilta varia*

Field characters. 13cm:5.0in Breeding male: *black and white striped crown, face and back;* two white wing-bars; *black throat;* breast and abdomen white with black streaks; under tail-coverts white with black spots. Breeding female: buffy ear coverts and sides; streaking reduced on underparts; *throat white* as in immature male.

Range. Eastern North America; winters in southern United States, Bahamas, the West Indies, Central and northern South America.

Cayman habitat. Mangrove; inland and littoral woodland; urban areas.

Habits. Song: *weezee weezee,* repeated in long series; call: loud *pink.* Creeps along the branches and boles of trees, exploring under the bark for insects.

Status. Common winter visitor in the three Islands, August to May.

AMERICAN REDSTART *Setophaga ruticilla*

Field characters. 13cm:5.0in Breeding male: dramatic black plumage with *brilliant orange red patches on wings, sides of breast and tail;* white abdomen and under tail-coverts. Breeding female: grey head; olive grey upperparts; orange replaced by *smaller yellow patches;* whitish underparts. Immature male resembles female until December when black spots appear on the throat and breast and yellow patches deepen to orange. Immature female: head olive; yellow on wing often absent.

Range. North America; winters in southern United States, the West Indies, Central America and South America.

Cayman habitat. Mangrove; woodland and bushland; urban/littoral areas.

Habits. Very active; known as the 'butterfly bird' due to its fluttering tumbling flight; perches briefly, and fans tail. Call: *chit;* song: *zwe zee zee zee zee (rising).*

Status. Fairly common to common winter visitor in the three Islands, August to May. Females and immatures predominate.

PROTHONOTARY WARBLER   *Protonotaria citrea*

Field characters. 14cm:5.5in Male: *golden head, neck and throat to abdomen;* under tail-coverts white; mantle greenish; wings and tail blue grey; unmarked wings. Female: similar except crown and nape greenish yellow. Both: black eye; long black bill.

Range. Eastern North America; winters to Central America and northern South America, rare in the West Indies.

Cayman habitat. Mangrove; woodland; urban/littoral areas.

Status. Rare passage migrant in the three Islands, August to October, and March to early May.

WORM-EATING WARBLER   *Helmitheros vermivorus*

Field characters. 13cm:5.0in Distinctive striped head pattern: *two black lateral stripes separating cinnamon crown stripe and superciliary;* long black eye-line; olive brown upperparts; unmarked wings; face and underparts buffy with cinnamon wash; pale legs. Sexes alike.

Range. Eastern United States; winters to the Greater Antilles, Bahamas and Central America.

Cayman habitat. In all habitats including areas of secondary growth.

Habits. Shy, remains in cover at low elevations, often hard to see; call: *chit* in a buzzing series.

Status. Fairly common winter visitor in the three Islands, August to April.

SWAINSON'S WARBLER   *Limnothlypis swainsonii*

Field characters. 13cm:5.0in Plain brownish back and unmarked wings; red brown crown; *wide pale superciliary stripe;* dark eye-line; yellowish white underparts; long bill; *pale legs.* Sexes alike.

Range. Southeastern United States; winters to the Greater Antilles, Bahamas and Central America.

Status. Very rare winter and passage migrant, September to April.

OVENBIRD   *Seiurus aurocapillus*

Field characters. 15cm:6.0in Large rounded warbler; *crown stripe orange, bordered by lateral black stripes;* face brownish; large eye accentuated by *white eye-ring;* upperparts olive brown, can appear light brown; underparts white with *dark brown spots and streaks on breast to flanks;* pale legs. Sexes alike.

Range. Eastern North America; winters southern United States, the West Indies, Central America and northern South America.

Cayman habitat. Moist woodland and bushland; mangrove; urban/littoral areas; damp Logwood, Grand Cayman.

Habits. Curious and tame; walks on ground and along low branches; flicks tail and carries it vertically with wings drooped. Song: *teach-er teach-er* repeated, in spring.

Status. Fairly common winter visitor in the three Islands, August to April.

NORTHERN WATERTHRUSH   *Seiurus noveboracensis*

Field characters. 14cm:5.5in Dark olive brown upperparts; unmarked wings; yellowish superciliary stripe; *dark* *eye-line;* brownish ear coverts; *brown spots on throat* and brown streaks on straw yellow underparts; pale legs. Sexes alike. Immature: yellowish wash on entire underparts.

Range. Northern North America; winters in Florida, Bahamas, the West Indies, Central and South America.

Cayman habitat. In cover in mangrove and Buttonwood swamps; also moist woodland; Logwood, Grand Cayman; arriving migrants in littoral areas.

Habits. Largely terrestrial; inquisitive; call: *pink,* repeated at intervals; bobs head and tips tail.

Status. A common winter visitor, Grand Cayman and Little Cayman; fairly common though restricted in habitat, Cayman Brac; August to early June, the majority depart in April.

LOUISIANA WATERTHRUSH   *Seiurus motacilla*

Field characters. 15cm:6.0in Very similar to Northern Waterthrush, but larger bill; *broader white superciliary stripe widens behind the eye;* streaked *white underparts* custard yellow to tan on sides and flanks; throat usually *white and unspotted.* Legs pink. Sexes alike.

Range. Eastern United States; winters in Florida, Bahamas, the West Indies, Central and northern South America.

Cayman habitat. Out of cover, near mangrove edge, beside ponds or close to moving water (shallow MRCU canals at the edge of North Sound).

Status. Rare winter visitor in the three Islands, July to April.

KENTUCKY WARBLER   *Oporornis formosus*

Field characters. 14cm:5.5in Male: olive green upperparts; unmarked wings; yellow underparts and under tail-coverts; blackish forehead and crown; *yellow superciliary curves around eye forming a partial ring; black sides to neck contrast with yellow throat.* Female: similar, except black greatly reduced. Immature: brownish; blackish markings, sometimes absent.

Range. Eastern United States; winters to Central and northern South America.

Cayman habitat. Urban/littoral areas.

Status. Very rare passage migrant, casual in winter, in the three Islands, October to April.

COMMON YELLOWTHROAT   *Geothlypis trichas*

Field characters. 13cm:5.0in Breeding male: olive brown upperparts; unmarked wings; wide *black mask across eyes to sides of neck, bordered by ashy grey band across crown;* bright yellow underparts except for *whitish abdomen and buffy sides.* Breeding female: mask absent, olive face with dusky ear coverts; duller than male; pale eye-ring. Immature: incomplete white eye-ring; olive face, blackish shows on face of males; absence of yellow superciliary distinguishes it from the Kentucky Warbler. All: pale legs.

Range. North America; winters in the southern breeding range, Bahamas, Greater Antilles and Central America to Panama.

Cayman habitat. Prefers secondary mangrove and Buttonwood; also woodland and bushland.

Habits. Call: *chur chur;* song: loud distinctive *witchery-witchery.*

Status. Fairly common to common winter resident in the three Islands, September to May.

HOODED WARBLER   *Wilsonia citrina*

Field characters. 14cm:5.5in Adult and immature male: *black hood extends to upper breast;* yellow fore-crown and face. Female: blackish olive crown and nape; yellow face and throat, may have reduced blackish green hood. All: greenish upperparts; unmarked wings; yellow underparts; tail white underneath.

Range. Southeastern North America; winters in Central America.

Status. Rare passage migrant and very rare winter visitor in the three Islands, September to March.

SUB-FAMILY COEREBINAE, BANANAQUITS. Small birds related to Warblers, found throughout the West Indies, occurring as different geographical sub-species. Sexes alike.

BANANAQUIT (Bananabird)   *Coereba flaveola*
   Plates 70, 71

Field characters. 12cm:4.5in Adult: upperparts dull black, except for yellow rump; *wide white superciliary;* black eye-line to nape; *red skin at base of downcurved bill; greyish white throat; bright lemon yellow breast;* whitish abdomen and under tail-coverts; *white rectangle on closed wing edge;* white spots on outer tail. Sexes alike. Immature: greyish brown upperparts; buffy under-parts, may have yellowish patches; greyish yellow superciliary stripe.

Range. Cayman Islands, West Indies (absent from Cuba), Central and South America.

Cayman habitat. Dry bushland preferred, but forages and breeds in all habitats.

Habits. Our most common passerine; forages on insects, fruits and nectar from flowers (feeds through petals) and trees (Logwood, Buttonwood, Pop-nut). Prolific, breeding throughout the year with peaks in spring and summer, constantly building round woven nests with entrance at side, used for roosting and breeding, clutch of 2–3, young fledge after 28 days. Song: unmusical churring 8–12 syllable *tse tse tse sweet tse tse sweet tse tse tse*, often conversational, other times urgent; call: *quit.*

Status. Very common to abundant breeding resident in the three Islands. An endemic subspecies *C. f. sharpei* (Cory).

SUB-FAMILY THRAUPINAE, TANAGERS. Frugiverous; found throughout tropical Americas. Male is brightly coloured. One breeding resident and two regular migrants occur. See Appendix 2.

STRIPE-HEADED TANAGER (Bastard cock)
Spindalis zena **Plates 72, 73**

Field characters. 20cm:8in Adult male: black head with *broad white superciliary and malar stripe;* small horn coloured bill; chin whitish; *black line separates malar stripe from throat; throat, upper breast, collar across hindneck, orange chestnut; rump and upper tail-coverts brownish orange;* upper-back greenish yellow; lower breast yellow; abdomen sides and under tail-coverts greyish white. Large white patch on wing coverts; black wing feathers broadly edged with white; tail black outer feathers with white margins. Our most brightly coloured endemic bird. Female: drab; *greyish olive upperparts;* greyish olive underparts; *greyish white superciliary* and rump; olive grey wings with pale edges to wing feathers; *whitish square on closed wing.* Immature male: resembles female except superciliary, malar stripe, wing coverts patch and edges to wing feathers are white; lower breast yellowish.

Range. Cayman Islands, Greater Antilles, Bahamas, Cozumel Island, Florida.

Cayman habitat. Breeds in woodland and bushland and forages in all habitats.

Habits. Usually in pairs. Call: *tweep*; song: slight warble, 8 to 9 syllables *tswee tswee tswee tswee,* rising and increasing in volume then falling; sings constantly in spring and throughout the summer. Very small cup nest, clutch 2–3 spotted, April to August.

Status. Fairly common breeding resident, Grand Cayman only. An endemic subspecies *S. z. salvina* (Cory).

SUMMER TANAGER *Piranga rubra*

Field characters. 19cm:7.5in Male: *entirely poppy red, winter and summer;* long heavy straw bill; unmarked wings. Female: greenish olive face and upperparts; yellowish underparts. Immature male: patched with red, increases to full plumage by second spring; bill dark.

Range. North America; winters to Central and South America, casual in Cuba and the Bahamas.

Cayman habitat. Urban/littoral and littoral areas.

Habits. Sings in migration, strong and melodious like an oriole but not as fluid; call: *pit-tuh pit-i-tuh.*

Status. Rare passage migrant in the three Islands, September to November, sometimes becoming locally common in spring, March to May. Casual in winter.

SCARLET TANAGER *Piranga olivacea*

Field characters. 18cm:7in Breeding male: *brilliant scarlet head and body contrasting with glossy black wings and tail;* large bill. Breeding female: similar to Summer Tanager, except *wings darker;* olive-green upperparts; pale yellow underparts. Immature and fall moulting male: greenish yellow patched with red. Non-breeding male: resembles female but retains black wings and tail.

Range. North America; winters in South America.

Status. Rare passage migrant in the three Islands in littoral habitats, September to mid-November, and March to May.

SUB-FAMILY CARDINALINAE, CARDINALS, GROSBEAKS AND NEW WORLD BUNTINGS. All migrant species, also see Appendix 2.

ROSE-BREASTED GROSBEAK *Pheucticus ludovicianus*

Field characters. 20cm:8in Breeding male: *glossy black head, throat and upperparts* and tail; *black wings with two dramatic white* *wing-bars and rectangular patch on inner primaries;* white rump and underparts; *red breast* and under wing-coverts; very large pale bill; black, white and red wing pattern in flight. Breeding female: dark brown crown with whitish central and superciliary stripes; dark brown streaked upperparts; paler brown streaks on whitish breast and sides; two white wing-bars; rich yellow underwing coverts. (Female Stripe-headed Tanager has no crown stripe and is olive). Non-breeding male: resembles female but retains red underwings, diffuse red patches on breast and black and white pattern in flight.

Range. North America; winters to Central and northern South America, rarely in western Cuba.

Cayman habitat. Low elevations in secondary growth near woodland; urban/littoral areas.

Habits. Warbling song; call: *click.* Often perches near ground and flicks tail.

Status. Uncommon to locally fairly common passage migrant, very uncommon in winter in the three Islands, October to early May.

BLUE GROSBEAK   *Guiraca caerulea*

Field characters. 18cm:7in Breeding male: vivid *ultramarine blue plumage; two tan wing-bars on dark wings* (upper wing-bar wider and brighter in both adults); black lores and chin; heavy bluish conical bill. Breeding female: gingery brown upperparts with brighter *brown wing-bars;* pale throat; darker breast; pale bill; blue mottling on rump.Non-breeding male: brown edges to feathers; blue less vivid. Immature male in first winter: chestnut brown.

Range. North and Central America; winters in the breeding range to Panama, rarely in Cuba.

Cayman habitat. Urban areas and bushy growth; Australian Pines (*Casuarina* sp.) along the coast; secondary mangrove and Buttonwood.

Status. Rare to uncommon, occasionally locally fairly

common, passage migrant in the three Islands, most frequently March and April, also October and November. Irregular, no records in some years.

INDIGO BUNTING   *Passerina cyanea*

Field characters. 14cm:5.5in Breeding male: vivid *ultramarine blue plumage in sunlight; dark unmarked wings;* small conical bill. Non-breeding male: reddish brown with blue patches on rump, tail and wings. Female: brown upperparts, may have faint tan wing-bars; pale throat; buffy underparts. Immature male: reddish brown upperparts with *two brown wing-bars;* streaked underparts; resembles Blue Grosbeak, blue develops on shoulders, rump and tail early in first spring.

Range. North America; winters to the Greater Antilles, Bahamas, Central and northern South America.

Cayman habitat. Low second growth in disturbed habitats in littoral and urban/littoral areas; *Casuarina* trees.

Status. Fairly common passage migrant and uncommon winter visitor in the three Islands, October to May.

SUB-FAMILY EMBERIZINAE, NEW WORLD SPARROWS. Small seed-eating birds of muted colours. Two breeding residents and two migrants occur.

CUBAN BULLFINCH (Black sparrow)   *Melopyrrha nigra*
Plates 74, 75

Field characters. 14cm:5.5in Adult male: plumage entirely black except for *a white line along the closed wing,* shows as white secondaries in flight; white under wing-coverts; *heavy black bill.* Female: smaller, greyish black; less white on wing. Immature: charcoal; male becomes speckled with black in first spring; pale bill; white on wing absent.

Range. Grand Cayman and Cuba.

Cayman habitat. Breeds in woodland and bushland; mangrove; uncommonly in urban/littoral areas.

Habits. Adults shy, staying concealed except during breeding season; immatures very tame and curious. Song: clear buzzing whistle *zeet zeet zeet* as 3 to 6 level phrases followed by 6 to 8 phrases ascending in a fluting trill. Forages on hard fruits, e.g. Logwood, Buttonwood and Thatch Palm. Large round untidy nest, often with two side entrances, woven into fine branches, similar to Bananaquit, also used for roosting, clutch 2–4, March to July.

Status. Common breeding resident, Grand Cayman only. An endemic subspecies, *M. n. taylori* (Hartlet).

YELLOW-FACED GRASSQUIT (Grass bird) *Tiaris olivacea* **Plate 76**

Field characters. 10cm:4in Our smallest resident bird. Adult male: upperparts greyish olive green; *rich yellow superciliary stripe, throat, and curve along lower eye-lid;* black eye-line and sides of throat to black breast patch; sides, abdomen and under tail-coverts greyish; small bill. Female: brownish olive upperparts; pale yellow on narrow eyebrow and chin only. Immature: brownish olive with no yellow on face.

Range. Cayman Islands, Greater Antilles, Central and northern South America.

Cayman habitat. Disturbed habitats including gardens, open grassy fields, roadsides and scrub bushland.

Habits. Gregarious, in small flocks; our only resident low-level grass feeder; uses empty Bananaquit nests for roosting at night. Call: *quit;* song: high pitched grating *zee zee zee zee zee.* Breeds in all seasons with peaks in spring and summer; small round nests with entrance at the side, clutch 3 usual.

Status. A very common breeding resident in the three Islands.

SAVANNAH SPARROW *Passerculus sandwichensis*

Field characters. 13cm:5.0in Pale central crown stripe; yellow superciliary in front of eye, buffy behind; pale malar stripe; brown streaked upperparts; *white underparts streaked with brown on breast and flanks;* short tail, notched; pink legs.

Range. North America to Central America; North American birds winter to Central America, the Bahamas and Cuba.

Cayman habitat. Open grassland.

Status. Very rare, recorded in winter and spring up to 1984 in Grand Cayman; no recent records.

GRASSHOPPER SPARROW *Ammodramus savannarum*

Field characters. 13cm:5.0in Upperparts striped black, beige and tawny; flat dark brown crown with central whitish stripe; *prominent dark eye in unmarked buffy face;* partial superciliary stripe; golden lores; *plain cinnamon buff breast and white abdomen;* large pale bill; narrow dark pointed tail. Immature: pale throat, some streaking on breast and sides.

Range. Greater Antilles, North, Central and South America.

Cayman habitat. Grassland, bushy fields.

Habits. Song: resembles a grasshopper, *chip-zeeeeeeee,* a very unbird-like sound, from a post or tall grass stem. Usually remains hidden, unlike the Grassquit.

Status. Very rare in the three Islands, October to April. Earlier recorded as fairly common in winter and spring.

SUB-FAMILY ICTERINAE, NEW WORLD BLACK-BIRDS AND ORIOLES. Two endemic sub-species and two regular migrants recorded. One endemic sub-species is extirpated.

BOBOLINK   *Dolichonyx oryzivorus*

Field characters. 18cm:7.25in Breeding male: black plumage, back and wing feathers edged with pale brown; white scapulars and rump; *buff hindneck;* pointed tail; large conical bill. Appears black and white in flight. Non-breeding male and breeding female: crown striped black and cinnamon; cinnamon underparts with streaked sides; upperparts olive and dark brown with pale edges to feathers; resembles a large Grasshopper Sparrow.

Range. North America; winters in South America.

Cayman habitat. Secondary mangrove; *Typha* sp. swamps; tall grassland around airports and agricultural land.

Habits. Gregarious; often migrate in separate male and female flocks. Call: *chick.*

Status. Fairly common passage migrant in the three Islands, September to October and April to May.

GREATER ANTILLEAN GRACKLE (Cling cling, Ching ching)   *Quiscalus niger*   **Plate 77**

Field characters. 27cm:11in Adult male: *entirely glossy blue black; bright yellow iris;* sharply pointed conical bill; *long, deeply keeled tail.* Female: smaller and less glossy; tail reduced; yellow iris. Immature: dull brownish black; *dark iris;* tail flat; appears to be a different species.

Range. Cayman Islands, Greater Antilles.

Cayman habitat. Breed in large colonies throughout the mangrove around North Sound, Grand Cayman; flocks of 2,000 or more birds roost together in late summer. Pairs and small groups also breed in littoral areas; forages in most habitats.

Habits. Gregarious. Aggressive, robs nests of eggs and nestlings, especially Bananaquits; also eats lizards and dragonflies. Many different calls include: single *click* and a 4 syllable conversational rasping with feathers fluffed out; song: fluting series. Breeds March to July after prolonged nest building; one or two clutches of 3 to 4.

Status. A breeding resident. The endemic sub-species *Q. n. caymanensis* (Cory) is abundant, Grand Cayman. The sub-species *Q. n. bangsi* (Peters) is very common, Little Cayman; it has been extirpated in Cayman Brac.

JAMAICAN ORIOLE   *Icterus leucopteryx*

Field characters. 21cm:8.25in *Black forehead, lores, and throat to front of breast;* rest of underparts bright yellow; back and crown dull yellow; wings and tail black; *large white wing coverts patch;* bill and feet black.

Range. Jamaica, San Andreas, formerly Grand Cayman.

Status. Extirpated. Previously an endemic sub-species, *I. l. bardi*, inhabited woodland and gardens in Grand Cayman only; it was last recorded between 1965–1967 in George Town.

NORTHERN ORIOLE   *Icterus galbula*

Field characters. 22cm:8.5in Male: *black head, back, breast* and tail; black wings edged with white; *orange rump, underparts and outer sides of tail.* Female: olive brown or greyish upperparts and tail; blackish olive on head; throat, breast and rump dull orange yellow; two white wing-bars. Immature male: resembles female, only brighter, becoming marked with black in first spring; immature female: upperparts lighter, olive grey not blackish.

Range. North America; winters in the Greater Antilles, Central and northern South America.

Cayman habitat. Urban and urban/littoral areas.

Status. Rare passage migrant in the three Islands, mainly in September and April.

APPENDIX I

Check-list of breeding birds showing status and distribution in the Cayman Islands. One recently extinct species and one extirpated species are included.

Species	Grand Cayman	Cayman Brac	Little Cayman
Waterbirds			
Pied-billed Grebe	BR	R	BR
White-tailed Tropicbird	SB	SB	—
Brown Booby	—	BR	—
Red-footed Booby	—	—	BR
Magnificent Frigatebird	R	—	BR
Least Bittern	R(B)	—	—
Snowy Egret	BR	R	IB
Little Blue Heron	IB	R	IB
Tricolored Heron	BR	R	IB
Cattle Egret	R(B)	IB	IB
Green Heron	BR	BR	BR
Yellow-crowned Night-Heron	BR	BR	BR
West Indian Whistling-Duck	BR	BR	BR
Purple Gallinule	BR	—	—
Common Moorhen	BR	BR	BR
Black-necked Stilt	BR	BR	BR
Willet	BR	BR	BR
Least Tern	SB	SB	SB
Landbirds			
White-crowned Pigeon	BR	BR	BR
White-winged Dove	BR	R	BR
Zenaida Dove	BR	BR	BR
Common Ground-Dove	BR	BR	BR
Caribbean Dove	BR	F	—
Cuban Parrot	BR	BR	e
Mangrove Cuckoo	BR	BR	BR
Smooth-billed Ani	BR	BR	BR
Barn Owl	BR	BR	BR
Antillean Nighthawk	SB	SB	SB
West Indian Woodpecker	BR	—	—
Northern Flicker	BR	F	—

226

Species	Grand Cayman	Cayman Brac	Little Cayman
Caribbean Elaenia	BR	BR	BR
La Sagra's Flycatcher	BR	—	—
Gray Kingbird	S(B)	SB	SB
Loggerhead Kingbird	BR	BR	e
Grand Cayman Thrush	E	—	—
Red-legged Thrush	—	BR	—
Northern Mockingbird	BR	BR	BR
Thick-billed Vireo	BR	BR	e
Black-whiskered Vireo	SN	SB	SB
Yucatan Vireo	BR	—	—
Yellow Warbler	BR	BR	BR
Vitelline Warbler	BR	BR	BR
Bananaquit	BR	BR	BR
Stripe-headed Tanager	BR	F	—
Cuban Bullfinch	BR	F	—
Yellow-faced Grassquit	BR	BR	BR
Greater Antillean Grackle	BR	e	BR
Jamaican Oriole	e	—	—

IB	intermittent breeding
BR	breeding proved, resident throughout the year
R	resident throughout the year, not breeding
R(B)	resident throughout the year, breeding probable, not proved
SB	summer visitor, breeding proved
S(B)	summer visitor, breeding not proved
SN	summer visitor, not breeding
E	extinct
F	fossil evidence
e	extirpated
—	absent

APPENDIX 2

A. Vagrant or very rare species not included in the main text

Vagrant: not expected in the Islands; outside their range.
Very rare: 1–10 records since 1886.
New records: sight records of new species have been seen by at least two observers or have been photographed; records below refer to single birds unless otherwise stated. Few observers at sea, along with geographical isolation, almost certainly account for the paucity of seabirds records.

CBC = Cayman Bird Club member
( ) = published records

BLACK-CAPPED PETREL　*Pterodroma hasitata*
　At sea off GC, April 1961 (Bond).
GREATER SHEARWATER　*Puffinus gravis*
　GC: shore, West Bay, June 1992; CBC, Roberts and Cooksley.
MASKED BOOBY　*Sula dactylatra*
　CB: a pair, bluff, 16 January 1984; bluff, 8 February 1994 (Bradley).
AMERICAN WHITE PELICAN　*Pelecanus erythrorhynchos*
　GC: three birds, North Sound, May 1977 (Bond).
ROSEATE SPOONBILL　*Ajaia ajaja*
　GC: 11 August 1971 (Johnston).
　CB: 19 January 1985 (Bradley).
　LC: 21 March–19 April 1985 (Bradley).
GREATER FLAMINGO　*Phoenicopterus ruber*
　GC: Barkers, August 1980, Sefton and Powery. Meagre Bay Pond 12–17 July 1983; Barkers, 6 November 1985 (Bradley).
　Unconfirmed reports. LC: South Hole Sound and westerly ponds, March, 1993, 1994.
CANADA GOOSE　*Branta canadensis*
　Unconfirmed report. LC: flock, Jackson's Pond, winter 1979, hunter to Bradley.
　Unconfirmed report. GC: large flock in flight, North Side, March 1983, to Bradley.

228

BLACK-BELLIED WHISTLING-DUCK *Dendrocygna autumnalis*
- GC: Red Bay pond, 4 August–September 1994; CBC, Benbow.

WOOD DUCK *Aix sponsa*
- LC: 8 birds, 17 February, 6 birds, Tarpon Lake, 28–30 March 1984 (Bradley).
- GC: 2 pairs introduced, North Sound Estates, September 1986.

GREEN-WINGED TEAL *Anas crecca*
- GC: Newlands, 6 November 1983 (Bradley).
- LC: Booby Pond, 28 November 1983 (Bradley).

WHITE-CHEEKED PINTAIL *Anas bahamensis*
- GC: pair, Meagre Bay Pond, 3 January–10 March 1985; pair, same site, 31 December 1986 (Bradley).

NORTHERN PINTAIL *Anas acuta*
- LC: 3 birds, Charles Bight Pond, 28 March 1984 (Bradley).

RING-NECKED DUCK *Aythya collaris*
- GC: 3 birds, Vulgunnes Pond, Barkers,19 November 1979 (Olson); Frank Sound, April–June, 1993, CBC.

RED-BREASTED MERGANSER *Mergus serrator*
- GC: Prospect swamp, 19 February 1989, Graham and observer; Malportas Pond, 8 February 1992, CBC, Marsden.

RUDDY DUCK *Oxyura jamaicensis*
- LC: Booby Pond, 26 June 1993, Gore (photographed).

MASKED DUCK *Oxyura dominica*
- GC: Bodden Town, 12 February 1972 (Wetmore).

AMERICAN SWALLOW-TAILED KITE *Elanoides forficatus*
- GC: North Sound, 23 August 1983 (Bradley); South Sound, 26 September 1992, CBC, Baillie and Davey; Lower Valley, 3 September 1994, CBC, Gore and Knox.
- CB: bluff, 14 March 1993, CBC.

SNOWY PLOVER *Charadrius alexandrinus*
- GC: George Town, 21 November 1992–4 January 1993, CBC, Gore and Dunkley.

229

AMERICAN AVOCET *Recurvirostra americana*
  CB: westerly ponds, 25 November 1985 (Bradley).
  GC: Barkers, 29 September 1993, Gore.
BAIRD'S SANDPIPER *Calidris bairdii*
  GC: Crystal Harbour, 4 October 1994, Marsden, CBC.
DUNLIN *Calidris alpina*
  GC: Barkers, 12 February 1983, Graham
       (photographed).
  CB: westerly ponds, 19 May 1986 (Bradley).
MARBLED GODWIT *Limosa fedoa*
  GC: North Sound, 14 September 1992, CBC, Bibby and
       Marsden.
LONG-BILLED DOWITCHER *Limnodromus scolopaceus*
  GC: 7 birds, North Side, 4 Jan–10 March 1984 (Bradley);
       Crystal Harbour, 2 September 1994, Bradley.
  LC: west end, 12–14 July 1975 (Diamond).
LONG-TAILED JAEGER *Stercorarius longicaudus*
  At sea off CB, April 1961 (Bond).
BROWN NODDY *Anous stolidus*
  GC: July 1889 (Cory).
BLACK-BILLED CUCKOO *Coccyzus erythropthalmus*
  GC: South Sound, 15 October 1993, CBC, Baillie.
BLACK SWIFT *Cypseloides niger*
  Unconfirmed report. GC: May and October 1985
       Bradley.
RUBY-THROATED HUMMINGBIRD *Archilochus colubris*
  Unconfirmed reports. GC: many reports to Johnston.
       (1965–1980) and Bradley (1982–1994).
ACADIAN FLYCATCHER *Empidonax virens*
  GC: South Sound, 30 September 1994, Knox, CBC.
LEAST FLYCATCHER *Empidonax minimus*
  GC: 1904 (Nicoll); February 1972 (Wetmore).
EUROPEAN STARLING *Sturnus vulgaris*
  CB: 16 March 1992 (Prescott).
FORK-TAILED FLYCATCHER *Tyrannus savana*
  GC: George Town, 9–15 October 1991; October 1992,
       CBC, Marsden.
PHILADELPHIA VIREO *Vireo philadelphicus*
  GC: South Sound, 16 October 1993, CBC, Baxter.

230

ORANGE-CROWNED WARBLER   *Vermivora celata*
Unconfirmed report. GC: South Sound, 17 October 1993, CBC, Baillie.

CANADA WARBLER   *Wilsonia canadensis*
GC: pond, 17 September 1993, CBC, Baillie; 21 September 1994, CBC, Baxter and Marsden.

YELLOW-BREASTED CHAT   *Icteria virens*
GC: 14 February 1973 (Wetmore).

SWALLOW-TANAGER   *Tersina viridis*
GC: Spotts, April 1982 (photograph to Bradley).

PAINTED BUNTING   *Passerina ciris*
GC: three birds, for three days in early April 1981, Quinn.

DICKCISSEL   *Spiza americana.*
GC: 20 April 1992, CBC, Baillie; 18 September 1994, CBC, Baxter and Marsden.

YELLOW-HEADED BLACKBIRD   *Xanthocephalus xanthocephalus*
GC: injured and died, North Side, September 1984-April 1985 (Bradley).

B. Introduced exotics: released or escaped cage birds not from the Islands. Since 1981 when the cage bird trade became popular, over 20 species of cage birds have been bred in captivity and over 30 species have been reported as escapees in the three Islands. The two species of dove and two species of parakeet, which are confirmed feral breeders, have been included in the text. Species listed below occur in small flocks in several areas, but breeding is unconfirmed; individual escapees are omitted.

CHUKAR   *Alectoris chukar*
GC: 20 birds, released East End, 1986; occasional reports.

WILD TURKEY   *Meleagris gallopavo*
GC: 12 birds, released East End, 1986; occasional reports.

HELMETED GUINEAFOWL   *Numida meleagris*
LC: introduced, 1975 (Diamond); no recent reports.

BLUE-AND-YELLOW MACAW   *Ara ararauna*
GC: escaped, George Town 1991; a pair, George Town 1994.

SULPHUR-CRESTED COCKATOO   *Cacatua galerita*
  GC: from 1986, George Town and West Bay, 1994.
BUDGERIGAR   *Melopsittacus undulatus*
  GC: escaped, small flocks, George Town to South Sound,
      1990, 1994; breeding unconfirmed.
COCKATIEL   *Nymphicus hollandicus*
  GC: small flocks, George Town, 1992–1994, and Savan-
      nah, 1994; breeding unconfirmed.
RED-MASKED CONURE   *Aratinga erythrogenys*
  GC: flock of three, George Town, 18 May 1994.
YELLOW-CROWNED PARROT   *Amazona ochrocephala*
  GC: flock of 5, South Sound, 1993, Bowman to Bradley;
      Bodden Town, flock of 4, 1994.

APPENDIX 3

Birding information and where to go

Join the Saturday morning birding walks with the Cayman Islands Bird Club; for meeting site contact John Benbow (Tel. office 949–7554, home –5348). The Club meets on the last Tuesday of each month at the National Trust building, off Eastern Avenue, George Town (Tel. 949–0121).

Be prepared for unexpected migrants due to the position of the Cayman Islands in the Caribbean Sea; new sightings please to Mrs P.E. Bradley, P.O. Box 907, Grand Cayman, Cayman Islands, West Indies.

A brief word of warning: after 10 am the tropical sun burns so carry a hat, sunscreen and a supply of water. Do not go into the swamps or walking on the pinnacled bluff limestone alone, go with a companion (and a compass) or guide; wear boots, a long sleeved shirt and long trousers. There are no poisonous snakes but there are several toxic plants including some vines and Maiden Plum (dark green shrub with leaflets sharply toothed), so it is best not to touch.

In view of the rapid pace of development in the Islands, sketch maps marking particular birding spots quickly become obsolete and have been omitted in this edition. Also new areas open up temporarily as mangrove is cleared, briefly providing good wader habitat. Therefore I have listed the best birding sites in the Islands in 1995, shown on Maps 1–3. Also I recommend using the Tourist map (price CI$5), as it is updated regularly and shows named development areas and new roads in the three Islands, and the remaining MRCU dyke roads and the extent of the present mangrove swamps in Grand Cayman.

Tropical islands provide relaxed enjoyable birding with good weather and sunshine almost guaranteed. It is best to begin early, after sunrise in summer before it gets hot, to watch feeding aggregates of herons and egrets and, in Cayman Brac and Little Cayman, seabirds departing from their colonies. Parrots, which are easy to see west of Savannah in Grand Cayman, are at their least active in the middle part of the day. Birds, especially the resident species, are very

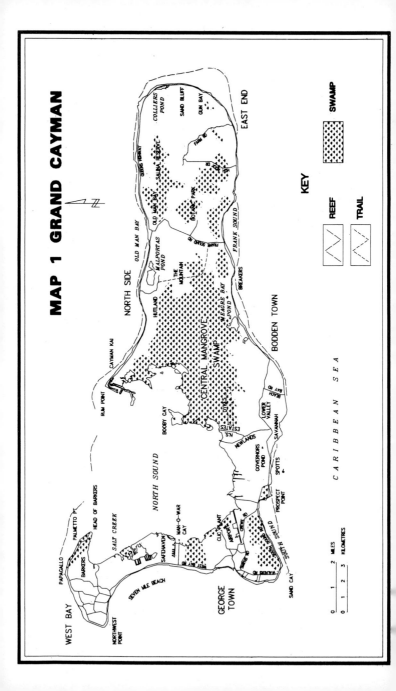

MAP 1 GRAND CAYMAN

KEY

SWAMP

REEF

TRAIL

WEST BAY
NORTHWEST POINT
PAPAGALLO
PALMETTO PT.
HEAD OF BARKERS
BARKERS
SALT CREEK
SEVEN MILE BEACH
GEORGE TOWN
SAND CAY
SOUTH SOUND
PROSPECT POINT
OLD ISLEVILLA
SPRING GDNS
WEST BAY RD
OLD CRICK
ARROWA
OLD PLANT
MAN-O-WAR CAY
SAFEHAVEN
NORTH SOUND
RUM POINT
CAYMAN KAI
BOOBY CAY
CENTRAL MANGROVE SWAMP
N.S. ESTATES
DYKES
NEWLANDS
GOVERNORS POND
SPOTTS
LOWER VALLEY
SAVANNAH
BEACH BAY RD
BODDEN TOWN
BREAKERS
MEAGRE BAY POND
THE MOUNTAIN
HUTLAND
MALPORTAS POND
OLD MAN BAY
NORTH SIDE
QUEENS HIGHWAY
BOTANIC PARK
FRANK SOUND
FRANK SOUND RD
FARM RD
SALINA RESERVE
COLLIERS POND
SAND BLUFF
GUN BAY
EAST END

CARIBBEAN SEA

0   1   2   MILES
0   1   2   3   KILOMETRES

approachable and easy to find using the habitat areas in the Introduction and the list of sites below.

Grand Cayman: Map 1; also Tourist map

1.   Barkers swamp. From Hog Sty Bay, George Town, drive up West Bay Road parallel to Seven Mile Beach to West Bay. Turn right into Town Hall Road and follow signs to Papagallo. Pass the restaurant and Villas Papagallo, enter the road along the northern coast passing Palmetto Point to Head of Barkers, the extreme northeast point of Grand Cayman. In 1995 the road continues on a track bordering North Sound, but care must be exercised as this area is scheduled for development and the dyke roads will be cut when dredging begins, entailing reversing a vehicle for a long distance. The inner MRCU dyke roads of the swamp to the left must be explored on foot. The mangrove, ponds, canals and shoreline are favoured areas for herons (especially the Yellow-crowned Night-Heron), ducks, migrant shorebirds, gulls and terns, vagrants e.g. flamingos, woodpeckers, raptors and migrant warblers.

2.   There are many areas between the West Bay Road and North Sound, all scheduled for development: (a) Salt Creek dyke roads, at present entered by the turn after the Yacht Club (opposite Tarquyn Manor), on the left is the entrance to the MRCU dyke roads. Explore the roads on foot, look for feeding aggregates of Snowy Egrets and Tricolored Herons. (b) Around the perimeter of the Safe Haven golf course to North Sound is good for migrant shorebirds. (c) Look for migrant warblers and buntings in the stands of *Casuarina* sp. trees along both sides of West Bay Road.

3.   Man O' War Cay. On West Bay Road, turn right into Palm Heights Drive beside the Clarion Hotel, follow the road east through the Snug Harbour Estate to North Sound. The mangrove covered Cay offshore is a roost for Magnificent Frigatebirds and herons and egrets in winter.

4.   Marl Pits. From Hog Sty Bay, George Town, take Shedden Road out of town, cross into North Sound Road at the

Eastern Avenue traffic lights; follow the road to the CUC generating plant, turn left along the perimeter fence to cat-tail fringed ponds and open land. Behind are the extensive flooded marl pits at the edge of North Sound, and ponds by the sewage farm. Look for ducks, migrant shorebirds, vagrant waterbirds, breeding Least Terns and Black-necked Stilt from April to September, woodpeckers, and flocks of grackles going to their summer roosts.

5. Back of South Sound swamp. On Smith Road turn into Robert Thompson Way and cross the brackish Half Way Pond swamp (Least Bitterns resident), keep bearing right following the main road; this is disturbed habitat (urban, secondary growth, agricultural land) and small areas of woodland, bushland and Logwood backed by mangrove. Look for migrant warblers, vireos and tanagers and resident landbirds. Continue to the perimeter of school playing fields and schools, and exit onto Walkers Road between two churches.

6. South Sound to Prospect Point. The littoral habitat (Sea-grape, Almond and *Casuarina*) along coast road is favoured by migrant warblers, grosbeaks, buntings and tanagers. Gulls and terns, herons, pelicans, frigatebirds and osprey are regular in the sound. Join the main Crewe Road/Red Bay Road going east, turn right into Prospect Point Road (one way). This area of mangrove, littoral woodland and rocky headland is excellent for terrestrial and wetland birds, including rare shorebirds in winter.

7. Governor's Pond. Continue east on the main road which becomes Jackson Drive then Poinciana Drive. Turn left into Spotts-Newlands Road, turn first right and the fenced Governor Michael Gore Sanctuary is 50 metres on the left. This area has many fresh to brackish water ponds where the Pied-billed Grebe and Purple Gallinule breed and Least Bittern is resident.

8. Central Mangrove Swamp. At Savannah crossroads, turn into Newlands Road, in approximately 1.3 miles turn right into North Sound Estates. Follow the paved road, turn right into Rackley Boulevard East, continue straight ahead around the outer border of the Estates, opposite Simons

Road turn right into the MRCU dyke roads and explore on foot. The migrants include warblers, raptors, tanagers and buntings; the indigenous birds include herons and egrets, pigeons and doves, woodpeckers, flycatchers including La Sagra's Flycatcher and parrots guaranteed morning and evening!

9.   Beach Bay Road. Small areas of woodland on bluff limestone remain where it is possible to see most breeding land birds including the White-crowned Pigeon, Zenaida Dove, both species of woodpeckers.

10.   Meagre Bay Pond, a protected area, and Pease Bay Pond. Mangrove, lagoons and ponds east of Bodden Town on the main road. It is possible to walk behind the ponds in the dry season; look for rafts of Pied-billed Grebe, feeding aggregates of herons and egrets, ducks, rails, waders, Least Terns breeding, migrant terns; the surrounding mangrove is parrot roosting and breeding habitat and a heron roost.

11.   Botanic Park, Frank Sound Drive. National Trust property. Look for the Caribbean and Zenaida Doves, the Cuban Parrot and Bullfinch, Stripe-headed Tanager and both species of woodpeckers. There is a signed walking trail through the mosaic of micro-habitats. Present hours: 7.30am-6.0pm, check with the Trust.

12.   The Mountain Reserve. Woodland and bushland on bluff limestone, the reserve is owned and managed by the National Trust for the Cayman Islands. Twice daily guided walks along the trail can be booked through the National Trust; a robust walk, not for the very unfit! Look for the White-crowned Pigeon, Caribbean Dove, Zenaida Dove, the parrot and resident and migrant landbirds.

13.   Hutland. Sign-post on the main road to Cayman Kai. Look for breeding birds including the Caribbean Dove and the Mangrove Cuckoo. The West Indian Whistling-Ducks flock at Willie Ebanks' farm close to Malportas Pond.

14.   High Rock Quarry Road loop to John McLean's Drive, East End. The habitat is bushland, agricultural land, button-

wood swamp and small areas of woodland. Look for resident and migrant landbirds including the vireos and flocks of parrots.

15.   Collier's Pond past Sand Bluff. Look for ducks and rare shorebirds.

16.   Take Frank Sound Drive north to Old Man Bay, turn right to go east along the Queen's Highway. There are three roads off the Highway inland; the habitat is mahogany woodland, mango plantations, agricultural land and dry bushland. Look for doves, cuckoos, the parrot, resident and migrant vireos, warblers and tanagers.

17.   East End Trail, Great Bluff. About 4.3 miles from Old Man Bay going east, park the car and walk up the path marked East End Trail through dry bushland habitat on bluff limestone. Look for endemic landbirds and migrant warblers.

Cayman Brac, Map 2

1.   Westerly ponds. Look for all species of waterbirds as this is one of the best sites in the Islands for uncommon species, including ibis, whistling-ducks, rails and shorebirds.

2.   West end, southwest of the airport. Look for osprey, falcons, Upland Sandpiper, swallows in the open land and migrant warblers in the mangrove fringe.

3.   Salt Water Pond to the Marshes. Scattered small wetlands in disturbed habitat. Look for herons and egrets, rails, migrant shorebirds including Killdeer; Black-necked Stilt, Willet and Least Tern breed in the Pond in summer; migrant warblers occur in the mangrove.

4.   Coastal and urban/littoral, southwest. Around the hotels and condos is an excellent site for uncommon migrant grosbeaks, buntings, tanagers, warblers and vireos, and breeding birds (ani, mockingbird and bananaquit). The Magnificent Frigatebird, herons and egrets, shorebirds and gulls and terns occur on the beach, boat docks and fringing reefs.

5.   South Side Road East and West, along the coastal plain. Look for the Barn Owl, Red-legged Thrush, Caribbean Elaenia, and Turkey Vulture at the extreme south east end. Up on the edge of the bluff a few pairs of Brown Booby breed in winter; two Masked Booby, which have been resident since 1984, are often seen.

6.   North coast, Creek to Spot Bay. Similar species to 4 above, also feeding flocks of parrots, and a colony of the White-tailed Tropicbird on the face of the bluff from January to September.

7.   Bluff Path to the Lighthouse, a walking trail. Drive to Spot Bay, walk on the path to the base of the bluff, climb up to the top of the bluff (stopping to admire the view: Plate 8) and follow the walking trail east to the Lighthouse (there is also a sealed road). Look for the frigatebird, Gray Kingbird in summer, doves, Mangrove Cuckoo, Red-legged Thrush and Northern Mockingbird. Along the extreme northeast bluff looking down, Brown Boobies can be seen with young in the breeding season on the sides and the rocky outcrops of the bluff.

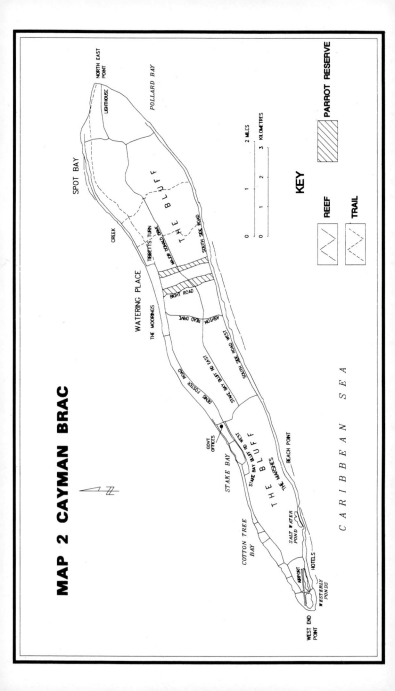

8. The eastern bluff to the lighthouse. From the coastal plain, turn up Ashton Reid Drive and into Major Donald Drive. This road runs along the centre of the bluff passing through areas of primary woodland and bushland on bluff limestone, agricultural land (look for West Indian Whistling-Duck here and in bushland) and into dry habitat (Thatch palm and cacti predominate) on the approach to the light-house. There are several walking trails and new roads which cross the Drive north to south. The first trail, the Bight Road, borders one of two areas of parrot breeding habitat owned and managed by the National Trust; there is a walking trail on the south side of this land; the Loggerhead Kingbird and Black-whiskered Vireo also breed here. Parrots, the Red-legged Thrush, migrant vireos and warblers can be seen throughout the bluff. The Thick-billed Vireo and Vitelline Warbler also occur in bushland, while the Cattle Egret, ani, Palm Warbler and Yellow-faced Grassquit prefer open habitat along the road.

9. The western bluff. Turn off Ashton Reid Drive into Stake Bay Bluff Road East. This road passes through woodland and bushland; it joins Stake Bay Bluff Road West and Quarry Road exiting at Cotton Tree Bay on the northern coast. The species here are similar to 8 above; the middle part of Stake Bay Road East is good parrot habitat, as are the trees at the base of the bluff at the Government Offices on the north coast.

MAP 3 LITTLE CAYMAN

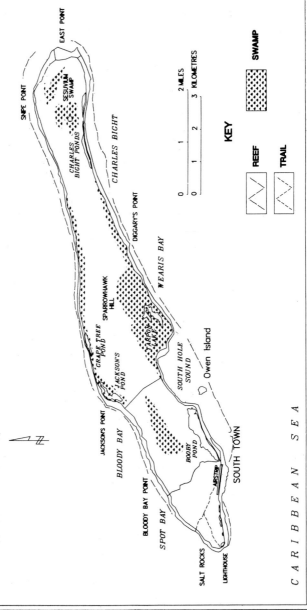

EAST POINT

SNIPE POINT

SESUVIUM SWAMP

CHARLES BIGHT PONDS

CHARLES BIGHT

DIGGARY'S POINT

WEARIS BAY

SPARROWHAWK HILL

GRAPE TREE POND

JACKSON'S POND

JACKSON'S POINT

BLOODY BAY

TARPON LAKE

SOUTH HOLE SOUND

Owen Island

BLOODY BAY POINT

SPOT BAY

BOOBY POND

AIRSTRIP

SOUTH TOWN

SALT ROCKS

LIGHTHOUSE

C A R I B B E A N   S E A

KEY

0	1	2 MILES

| 0 | 1 | 2 | 3 KILOMETRES |

REEF

TRAIL

SWAMP

Little Cayman, Map 3

1.   Booby Pond Sanctuary. The main birding attractions are the breeding colonies of Magnificent Frigatebird and 3,500 pairs of the Red-footed Booby on the landward side of the pond. The colonies can be observed from across the pond and from the observation tower.

2.   Walking trails at west end. Enter at the Lighthouse and at Salt Rocks, the trails exit on the landward side of the old airstrip. An earlier north-south path across the western part of the Island is being widened as a road; it passes through representative habitats and most species of landbirds occur. Take the road north (inland) at the western end of Booby Pond across the island exiting opposite Spot Bay. Look for Vitelline Warblers, doves, and migrant warblers.

3.   Waterbirds occur on all the roadside lagoons and ponds and migrant warblers and vireos are found in the mangrove fringe. Look for herons and egrets, stilts, the resident West Indian Whistling-Duck, migrant ducks and shorebirds and breeding Least Terns in summer (Jackson's Pond). Tarpon Lake, which is still recovering from the effects of the 1988 hurricane, has migrant ducks. Gulls, pelicans, herons and egrets and migrant shorebirds occur around the coasts especially on the reef at Owen Island and around South Hole Sound, and cormorants and anhinga occur here after storms. A visit to the inland ponds and swamps requires the company of a local guide.

4.   Coastal littoral, especially from South Hole Sound west to Bloody Bay. Look for the Yellow-crowned Night-Heron, migrant kestrel and merlin, doves, migrant sapsucker, Caribbean Elaenia, ani, Gray Kingbird and Antillean Nighthawk in summer, Barn Owl, and endemic sub-species of grackle.

5.   The Bluff. On the north side before Jackson's Pond, turn inland on the road that bisects the Island; look for migrant warblers and vireos on the bluff. At Snipe Point on the east end climb the bluff and look for migrant warblers in the low dry vegetation.

MAP 4 REGIONAL LOCATION MAP

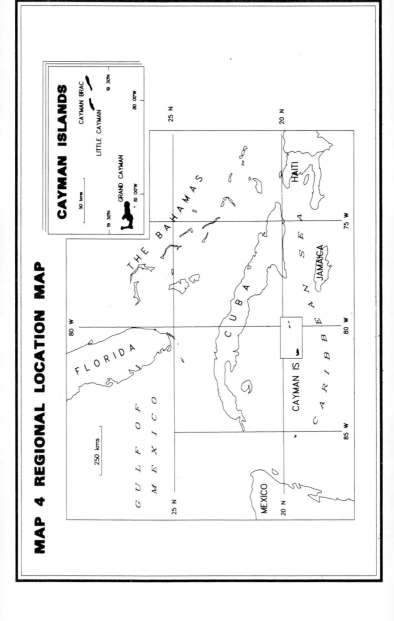

CAYMAN ISLANDS

LITTLE CAYMAN

CAYMAN BRAC

GRAND CAYMAN

50 kms

19 30'N
81 00'W

19 30'N
80 00'W

25 N

20 N

75 W

80 W

85 W

250 kms

FLORIDA

G U L F   O F
M E X I C O

25 N

20 N

MEXICO

THE BAHAMAS

C U B A

HAITI

JAMAICA

CARIBBEAN SEA

CAYMAN IS

Position of the Cayman Islands in relation to Cuba, Jamaica and Central America, Map 4

The three Islands are at the extreme western end of the Greater Antilles, lying 280 km (175 miles) north west of Jamaica and 240 km (149 miles) west of Cuba in the Caribbean Sea.

Grand Cayman is the largest of the Islands and the furthest west. It is 35 km (25 miles) long and 13 km (8 miles) wide. Position 19°20′ N; 81°20′ W.

Cayman Brac lies 133 km (79 miles) east north east of Grand Cayman; it is 19 km (12 miles) long and 3 km (2 miles) wide. Position 19°43′ N; 79°50′ W.

Little Cayman is the smallest of the three Islands and lies 8 km (5 miles) west of Cayman Brac. It is 16 km (10 miles) long and 1.7 km (1 mile) wide. Position 19°41′ N; 80°03′ W.

BIBLIOGRAPHY

American Ornithologists' Union, 1983, Check-list of North American Birds, 6th edition. American Ornithologists' Union. Allen Press, Kansas.

American Ornithologists' Union. 1989. Thirty-seventh Supplement to the American Ornithologists' Union Check-list of North American Birds. Auk 106: 532–538.

Arendt, W.J., T.A. Vargas Mora, and J.W. Wiley. 1980. White-crowned Pigeon: Status rangewide and in the Dominican Republic. Proc. Ann. Conf. S.E. Assoc. F & W Ag. 33:111–122.

Balat, F. and H. Gonzalez. 1982. Concrete data on the breeding of Cuban birds. Acta Sc. Nat. Brno, 16(8): 1–46.

Bangs, O. 1916. A collection of birds from the Cayman Islands. Bull. Mus. Comp. Zool. 60:(7) 303–320.

———. 1919. The races of *Dendroica vitellina* Cory. Bull. Mus. Comp. Zool. 62:(11) 493–495.

Banks, R.C. Original text for the new A.O.U. subspecies companion volume (in prep).

Barlow, J.C. 1978. Records of migrants from Grand Cayman Island. Bull. Brit. Ornith. Cl. 98(4): 144–146.

Blake, E.R. 1977. Manual of Neotropical Birds. Vol.2. Univ. Chicago Press.

Bond, J. 1934. The distribution and origin of the West Indian avifauna. Proc. Amer. Philos. Soc. 73: 341–349.

———. 1936. Handbook of Birds of the West Indies. 1st edition. Acad. Nat. Sci. Philadelphia.

———. 1939. Notes on birds from the West Indies and other Caribbean Islands. Notulae Naturae, Acad. Nat. Sci. Philadelphia 13: 1–6.

———. 1942. Additional Notes on West Indian Birds. Proc. Acad. Nat. Sci. Philadelphia. 94: 89–106.

———. 1948. Origin of the bird fauna of the West Indies. Wilson Bull. 60: 207–229.

———. 1950. Results of the Catherwood-Chaplin West Indies Expedition, 1948. Part 2. Birds of Cayo Largo (Cuba), San Andres and Providencia. Proc. Acad. Nat. Sci. Philadelphia. Vol C11: 43–68.

——. 1956. Check-list of Birds of the West Indies. Acad. Nat. Sci. Philadelphia.

——. 1957–1984. Second to twenty-sixth supplements to the Check-list of Birds of the West Indies (1956).

——. 1963. Derivation of the Antillean Avifauna. Proc. Acad. Nat. Sci. Philadelphia. 115:(4) 79–98.

——. 1966. Affinities of the Antillean Avifauna. Carib. J. Sci. 6 (3–4): 173–176.

——. 1978. Derivations and continental affinities of Antillean birds. In Gill, F.B.,(ed.) 'Zoogeography in the Caribbean'. Acad. Nat. Sci. Philadelphia, Special Publ. 13, pp. 119–128.

Bradley, P.E. 1984. Report in Gosse Bird Club Broadsheet 42:11.

——. 1985. Report in Gosse Bird Club Broadsheet 44:4.

——. 1986a. The Cayman Islands. In Scott, D. A., and Carbonell, M. (eds.): A Directory of Neotropical Wetlands. IUCN, Gland and Cambridge.

——. 1986b. A Census of *Amazona leucocephala caymanensis*, Grand Cayman and *Amazona leucocephala hesterna*, Cayman Brac. C.I. Gov. Tech. Pub. 1.

——. 1986c. Report in Gosse Bird Club Broadsheet 46:5.

——. 1995. The Avifauna of the Cayman Islands: an overview. In The Cayman Islands: Natural History and Biogeography. 1995. Kluwer Acad. Publ. The Netherlands.

——. in Arendt,W. Status of North American landbirds in the Caribbean region: a summary (in press).

Buden, D. W. 1985. New subspecies of Thick-billed Vireo (Aves: Vireonidae) from the Caicos Islands, with remarks on taxonomic status of other populations. Proc. Biol. Soc. Washington. 98: 591–597.

Brunt, M.A., and M.E.C. Giglioli. 1980. Cayman Islands Swamp maps, Sheets 1–3, 1:25,000 scale. Land Resources Centre, UK-O.D.A.

Brunt, M.A. 1984. Introduction. In G.R. Proctor 'Flora of the Cayman Islands'. Kew Bull. Add. Ser. X1, pp 1–67. HMSO. London.

Clapp, R.B. 1987. Status of the Red-footed Booby on Little Cayman Island. Atoll Res. Bull. No. 304. Smithsonian Inst.

Cory, C.B.C. 1886a. Descriptions of thirteen new species of birds from the island of Grand Cayman, W.I. Auk 3: 497–501.

——. 1886b. A list of birds collected on the island of Grand Cayman, W.I., by W.B. Richardson, during the summer of 1886. Auk 3: 501–502.

——. 1887. A new vireo from Grand Cayman, West Indies. Auk 4: 6–7.

——. 1889. A list of birds collected by Mr. C.J. Maynard in the islands of Little Cayman and Cayman Brac, West Indies. Auk 6: 30–32.

——. 1892. Catalogue of West Indian Birds. Publ. by the author, pp 163.

Cory, C.B. and C.E. Hellmayr. 1927. Catalogue of Birds of the Americas and the adjacent Islands. Vol X111. Part 5. Field Mus. Nat. Hist. Zool. Ser.

Cruz, A. and D.W. Johnston. 1979. Occurrence and feeding ecology of the Common Flicker on Grand Cayman Island. Condor 81(4): 370–375.

Delacour, J. 1954–1964. The Waterfowl of the World. Country Life Ltd. London. Vols. 1,2.

Diamond, A.W. 1980a. Ecology and species turnover of the birds of Little Cayman. Atoll Res. Bull. No. 241: 141–164. Smiths. Inst.

——. 1980b. The Red-footed Booby colony on Little Cayman: size, structure and significance. Atoll Res. Bull. No. 241: 165–170. Smiths Inst.

Downer, A. and R. Sutton. 1990. Birds of Jamaica. Cambridge University Press.

Eaton, S. W. 1953. Wood Warblers wintering in Cuba. Wilson Bull. 65(3): 169–174.

English, T.M. Savage 1912. Some notes on the natural history of Grand Cayman. Handbook of Jamaica for 1912, pp 598–600. Kingston.

——. 1916. Notes on some birds of Grand Cayman, West Indies. Ibis. ser 10, 4: 17–35.

Faaborg, J. R. 1985. Ecological Constraints on West Indian Bird Distribution. In Buckley, P.A., M.S. Foster, E.S. Morton, R.S. Ridgely, & F.G. Buckley (eds.) Neotropical Ornithology. A.O.U., Monog. No. 36: 621–653.

Fisher, A.K. and A. Wetmore. 1931. Report on birds recorded by the Pinchot Expedition of 1929 to the Caribbean and Pacific. Proc. U.S. Nat. Mus. 79: 1–66.

Garrido, O. H. and F. Garcia Montana. 1975. Catalogo de las Aves de Cuba. pp 149. Acad. de Ciencias de Cuba, La Habana.

Gorman, M. 1979. Island Ecology. Chapman and Hall, London.

Hancock, J. and J. Kushlan. 1984.The Herons Handbook. Croom Helm Ltd.

Harrison, P. 1983. Seabirds: an identification Guide. Croom Helm Ltd.

Hartert, E. 1896. Description of a new finch from the West Indies. Nov. Zool.3(3): 257.

Hayman, P.J. Marchant, and T. Prater. 1991. Shorebirds: an identification guide to waders of the world. Christopher Helm Ltd. London.

Hellmayr, C.E. 1935–40. Catalogue of Birds of the Americas. Vol.13 Field. Mus. Nat. Hist., Zool. Ser. Chicago.

Johnsgard, P.A. 1978. Ducks, Geese & Swans of the World. Univ. Nebraska Press, Nebraska.

Johnston, D.W. 1965. Grand Cayman Island in early May. Gosse Bird Club Broadsheet 5: 4–5.

——. 1969. The thrushes of Grand Cayman Island, B.W.I. Condor 71: 120–128.

Johnston, D.W., C.H. Blake, and D.W. Buden. 1971. Avifauna of the Cayman Islands. Quart.J. Florida Acad. Sci. 34(2): 141–156.

Johnston, D.W. 1974. Food of the Barn Owl on Grand Cayman, B.W.I. Quart. J. Florida Acad. Sci. 35 (4): 171–172.

——. 1975. Ecological analysis of the Cayman Islands avifauna. Bull. Florida State Mus. Biol.Sci. 19(5): 235–300.

Jones, B. The Geology of the Cayman Islands. In The Cayman Islands: Natural History and Biogeography. 1995. Kluwer Acad. Publ. The Netherlands.

Kidd, E.R.G. 1965. Grand Cayman. Jan 23–28 1964. Gosse Bird Club Broadsheet 4:3.

Lack, D. 1973. The number of species of hummingbirds in the West Indies. Evol. 27: 326–337.

——. 1976. Island Biology. Blackwell Sci. Publ., Oxford, pp 445.

Lanyon, W.E. 1967. Revision and probable evolution of the *Myiarchus* flycatchers of the West Indies. Bull. Amer. Mus. Nat. Hist. 136: 329–370.

Lowe, P.R. 1909. Notes on some birds collected during a cruise in the Caribbean Sea. Ibis, ser 9, 3:304–347.

——. 1911. On the birds of the Cayman Islands, West Indies. Ibis, ser.9 5:137–161.

MacArthur, R.H.& E.O. Wilson. 1967. The theory of Island Biogeography. Princeton Univ. Press, Princeton.

Mayr, E. 1946. History of the North American bird fauna. Wilson Bull. 58: 3–62.

Maynard, C.J. 1889. Description of a supposed new species of Gannet (*Sula coryi*) from Little Cayman. Contrib. to Sci., 1: 40–49.

Moore, A. G. 1985. Winter status of birds on Grand Cayman Island. Bull. Brit. Ornith. Cl. 105(1): 8–17.

Morgan, G.S. Fossil vertebrates from the Cayman Islands. In the Cayman Islands: Natural History and Biogeography. 1994. Kluwer Acad. Publ. The Netherlands.

Nelson, J.B. 1978. The Sulidae. Oxford Univ. Press. Oxford.

Nicoll, M.J. 1904. On a collection of birds made during the cruise of the 'Valhalla' R.Y.S. in the West Indies (1903–04). Ibis. Ser 8. 4: 555–591.

Noegel, R. 1974. The Cayman Brac Amazon. Avicult. Mag. 82: 202–208.

——. 1977. Captive Breeding of *Amazona leucocephala*. Avicult. Mag. 83:126–130.

——. 1980. *Amazona leucocephala*: Status in the wild and potential for captive breeding. In Conservation of New World Amazons. ICBP Tech. Pub. No.1, pp73–79.

——. 1983. Caribbean Island Amazons, Captive Breeding for Conservation, pp 187–192. Int. Found. for Conserv. of Birds, Los Angeles, Calif. Ed.A.C. Risser and F.S. Todd.

Olson, S.L., H.F. James, & C.A. Meister. 1981. Winter field notes and specimen weights of Cayman Island Birds. Bull. Brit. Ornith. Cl. 101 (3): 339–346.

Palmer, R.S. 1962–76. Handbook of North American birds. Vols 1–4. Yale Univ. Press, New Haven.

Patti, S.T., D.I. Rubenstein, and N. Rubenstein. 1974. Distribution notes on the Birds of Cayman Brac. Fla. Sci. 37(3): 155–156.

Paynter, R.A.Jr.1956. Birds of the Swan Islands. Wilson Bull. 68(2): 103–110.

Peters, J.L. 1921. A review of Grackles of the genus *Holoquiscalus*. Auk 38: 435–453.

Procter, G.R. 1984. The Flora of the Cayman Islands. Kew Bull. Add. Ser.XI. HMSO. London.

Richards, H.G. 1955. The Geological History of the Cayman Islands. Notulae Naturae. 284. Acad. Nat. Sci. Philadelphia.

Prescott, K. 1994. The birds of Cayman Brac and where to find them. National Trust for the Cayman Islands.

Ricklefs, R.E. and G.W. Cox. 1972. Taxon cycles in the West Indian avifauna. Amer. Nat. 106: 195–219.

Ridgway, R. 1887. Catalogue of a collection of birds made by Mr. Chas. H. Townsend on islands in the Caribbean Sea and in Honduras. Proc. U.S. Nat. Mus. 10: 572–597.

——. 1898. New Species of American Birds. Auk 15: 319–324.

Robertson, D. & L.F. Baptista.1988. White-shielded Coots in North America: a critical evaluation. Amer. Birds 42(5):1,241–1,246.

Schwartz, A. 1970 (1971). Subspecific variation in two species of Antillean birds. Quart. J. Fla. Acad. Sci. 33(3): 221–236.

Schwartz, A.& .F. Klinikowski. 1963. Observations on West Indian birds. Proc. Acad. Nat. Sci. Philadelphia. 115 (3): 53–77.

Short, L.L.1965. Variations in West Indian Flickers (Aves, Colaptes). Bull. Fla. State Mus. 10 (1): 1–42.

Steadman, D.W. & G.S. Morgan. 1985. A new species of Bullfinch (AVES: EMBERIZIDAE) from a late Quaternary cave deposit on Cayman Brac, West Indies. Proc. Biol. Soc. Washington 98(3): 544–553.

Stoddart, D.R. 1980a. Geology and Geomorphology of Little Cayman. Atoll Res. Bull. No. 241: 11–16. Smithsonian Inst. Washington.

Terborgh, J. 1973. Chance, habitat and dispersal in the distribution of birds in the West Indies. Evol. 27: 338–349.

Todd, W.E.C. 1916. The Birds of the Isle of Pines. Ann. Carnegie Mus. 10 (11):146–296.

Turner, A.and C.Rose.1989. Swallows & Martins. Christopher Helm Ltd, Kent.

Wiley, J.W. 1979. The White-crowned Pigeon in Puerto Rico: status, distribution, and movements. J. Wildl. Manage. 43: 402–413.

———. 1991. Status and conservation of parrots and parakeets in the Greater Antilles, Bahama Islands, and Cayman Islands. Bird Conservation International 1:187–214.

Wiley, J.W., Ground McCoy, D., Cross, S., Scharr, P., Burton, F., Ebanks-Petrie, G., Marsden, M., Butler, P., and Prescott, K. 1991a. Report on surveys of the Cayman Brac Parrot (*Amazona leucocephala hesterna*) on Cayman Brac, February 1991. George Town, Grand Cayman: National Trust for the Cayman Islands. (Unpub. Report).

Wiley, J.W., Gnam, R.S., Burton, F., Walsh, M., Weech, J., Strausberger, B., Marsden, M. Report on observations of the Cayman Brac Parrot (*Amazona leucocephala hesterna*) on Cayman Brac, June 1991. Report for the International Council for Bird Preservation. (in press).

Unpublished references

Bartsch, P. 1930. Field notes of visits to the Cayman Islands. Library of the Smithsonian Inst.

Bradley, P. E. Population counts of wetland birds on Grand Cayman, Cayman Brac, and Little Cayman, 1982–1986 (in prep).

Marsden, M. Records from Grand Cayman Island, 1989–1994. Cayman Islands Bird Club.

Wetmore, A. Field notes of his visits to Grand Cayman, 1972, 1973, 1975. Library of the Smithsonian Inst.

Recommended Books

Field guide to Birds of North America. National Geographic Society.

Field Guide to Birds East of the Rockies. Roger Tory Peterson. Houghton, Mifflin & Co.

Birds of the West Indies, James Bond. 5th edition 1985. Collins.

Warblers of the Americas. An Identification Guide. Jon Curson, David Quinn and David Beadle. 1994. A & C Black. London.

Due in 1996: Birds of the West Indian Region. Raffaele, H.A., J.W. Wiley, O.H. Garrido, R.L. Norton. Princeton.

ENGLISH AND LATIN INDEX

259